WHY I AM

A UNITARIAN

UNIVERSALIST

WHY I AM
A UNITARIAN
UNIVERSALIST

By

Jack Mendelsohn

BEACON PRESS   BOSTON

Copyright, 1964, by Jack Mendelsohn

First published as a Beacon Paperback in 1966
by arrangement with Thomas Nelson & Sons

Published simultaneously in Canada by Saunders of Toronto, Ltd.

All rights reserved under International and Pan-American Conventions

Beacon Press books are published under the auspices of the
of the Unitarian Universalist Association

Printed in the United States of America

International Standard Book Number: 0-8070-1199-1

9   8   7   6   5   4

PREFACE

IN *Why I Am A Unitarian*, published in 1960, I said: "As these words are being written, it seems probable that an official, organic union [of Unitarians and Universalists] will actually take place, thus producing one denomination in place of the present two. Administrative details . . . are still to be worked out; and, given the near-misses of the past, there is the possibility that we will yet go our separate, but cordial, ways. However, the climate for functional merger is favorable."

As one who believed firmly in the principle of Unitarian Universalist consolidation, it is immensely satisfying to report the merger of the American Unitarian Association and the Universalist Church of America as an accomplished and happy fact.

The Unitarian Universalist Association became a reality on May 11, 1961, in Boston, when the two historic liberal religious movements formally united. A century of parallel thought and action had resulted in philosophies and purposes so increasingly similar that by the 1950's the advantages of merger began to reduce obstacles. A step-by-step plan for complete union emerged from a welter of study groups and committees.

Union of Unitarian and Universalist youth organizations was achieved in 1953, with the establishment of Liberal Religious Youth. In 1954 a single staff for religious education was assigned to a temporary administrative unit called the Council of Liberal Churches. Two years later a Joint Merger Commission was formed. In October, 1959, at Syracuse, the Commission reported to simultaneous meetings of the two denominational bodies and won overwhelming approval for its proposals, which were then submitted for a plebiscite among all churches and fellowships. Decisive majorities voted approval. At meetings in May, 1960, concurrent votes of the Universalist General Assembly and the Unitarian Annual Meeting gave official sanction to full merger. The action was once again submitted to the individual congregations, resulting in a nearly unanimous vote of approval. The stage was now set for the historic decision in Boston in May, 1961, where the Unitarian Universalist Association was created, and Dr. Dana McLean Greeley was elected first president.

This new edition appears bearing proudly the recognition that I am no longer a Unitarian, but a Unitarian Universalist.

I look upon all minds as one family and upon all men as one race. Yet, there are differences in our thoughts and in our compacts with life. We are linked by robust bonds of intelligence, interest, need, and emotion. As much as possible, I want my life to be a pledge to likenesses and similarities. Still, we explore the less tangible realms of spirit in different ways. We come to terms with the universe by diverse paths.

Some are certain to be offended by this book's unorthodoxy. Others will be amused. Still others will experience a veritable surge of fellow feeling.

I apologize to those who are outraged, not because of the thoughts expressed, since they are honest and sincere enough, but simply because I do not enjoy causing anger. To those who are amused, I extend a hand in communion. I, too, am entertained by the presumption involved in the writing of this book. Those who recognize here many of their own articulate or inarticulate thoughts will know the joy of having their heresies confirmed.

There is room on the great adventure of religion for solutions independent of the traditional or neo-traditional creeds and symbolisms. There is space in the spectrum of spiritual life for interpretations other than those conventionally found in orthodox institutions.

My choice of Unitarian Universalist religion is a personal one, made consciously from alternatives, and does not in any way imply that we have a monopoly on the practice of liberalism in religion. I might have become a Hicksite Quaker, or a member of the Ethical Societies.

On the assumption, then, that what follows is one man's opportunity to spell out his reasons for being what he is, I dedicate this book to all who believe that true religion has nothing whatever to fear from honest thought and who honor the courage to question and the boldness to grow.

Jack Mendelsohn

Boston, Massachusetts

CONTENTS

WHY I AM

A UNITARIAN

UNIVERSALIST

ONE

BY WHAT HE IS

Man, like the generous vine, supported lives:
The strength he gains is from the embraces he gives.

ALEXANDER POPE, *Essay on Man*

MAN is glorious and happy," wrote William Ellery Channing, "not by what he has, but by what he is. He can receive nothing better or nobler than the unfolding of his own spiritual nature."

The Unitarian Universalist religion's gift to me has been the opportunity to unfold: the special joy of breaking out of the cocoon, of finding a greater freedom in the exercise of my intelligence and in the growth of my experience of love, beauty and justice.

A childhood is made of many things: sounds, smells, anticipations, tears, playgrounds, backfences. Mine was such a childhood, a compound of chance and purpose, marvel and misery. I remember with special warmth my grandfather who had been one of the earliest of the professional home-run hitters. It was he who guided my first nervous attempts at playing organized baseball. I remember the summer I fastened a chinning-bar on the back porch in the conviction it would help to stretch my body to the more than six feet of height I so desperately desired. I remember the hours I spent poring over my uncle's picture book of World War I, and the morbid fear I nursed that there might never be an-

13

other war in which I could perform heroic deeds. Such are the unpredictabilities of childhood! I was never any better than a Class D ballplayer. My great spurt of growth came in my fourteenth summer, when the chinning-bar was long forgotten. By the time we found ourselves in World War II, I was a confirmed pacifist.

As I look back over the tender years, there is little to prophesy the eventual turn of my life toward the ministry, except that I was an unrelenting reader. My room, to the dismay of my parents and later my grandparents, was forever strewn with books. At Christmas and birthdays there were only two kinds of gifts I really wanted: athletic equipment and books. As for religion, it was anything but a burden. None of my relatives pried into my religious thoughts, and I did very little prying of my own. My father was and is an uncomplicated person religiously, for whom theology is about as pressing a concern as witchcraft.

I worshipped my mother, and was never given the opportunity to grow beyond a small boy's craving for her approval and affection. She was statuesque, freckled, red-headed and very beautiful. Or so I remember. She was youthful. Even as a child, when anyone over twenty seemed ancient, I was deeply conscious of her youngness. She played the piano professionally and had begun to teach me. She cooked wonderful soups and often held me in her lap. I needed her terribly and was painfully aware of it.

One day I ran home from school. I was six and a first-grader in the old Morse School in Cambridge. The teacher left the room, whereupon the children exploded into a chaos of screaming, jumping and eraser throwing. Suddenly she was back, and I stood transfixed with an eraser in my hand. In a towering rage she pulled me from the room and ordered me to stand alone in the hall until she was ready to deal with me. I was the only culprit apprehended and humbled. Part of what I felt was fear, but a great part was outrage. In the face of massive injustice, I bolted from the corridor and ran home, where I knew there would be justice even though it would include punishment for my transgression. I ran to my mother and was not disappointed. She deprived me of several privileges for a few days, but she also took me back to school, hand in hand, where she charmed and soothed the distraught teacher and returned me honorably to my peers.

This is the mother I remember. For a time it was difficult for me to think of God as being anyone but a woman, like my mother.

Then life taught me something else.

I was eight, and shared a twin-bedded room with my sister, who is three years younger. I awoke in the darkness and peered into the hall where I caught a harrowing glimpse of my father helping my mother down the stairs. Her face was twisted with pain. It was the last time I ever saw her.

Years later I learned it was a miscarriage that took her to the hospital that night. My grandmother came the next morning and an air of mystery haunted the house. A few nights later I awakened again and heard my grandmother and father whispering. Soon they left. No one told me, but I knew what was happening. My sister slept, and I paced in the darkness of our parents' room, sobbing aloud, "She can't die. Oh, God, don't let her die!"

She did die, and at dawn my father returned to tell us how it happened. The cause, though it meant nothing to me at the time, was peritonitis. All that mattered to me was the loss of the most important person in the world. I was hurt and angry, desolate and resentful. For the first time in my life I had asked God for something. I had begged God for something! And God had turned and cracked me in the face, as I had seen parents strike some of my playmates.

From that moment religious questions have never been far from my thoughts. It may be a gift or a neurosis, but I have since been gripped with the habit of religious searching.

It would be wrong, however, to give the impression of youthful zealotry or intense concentration.

Soon after my mother's death, I went to live with my maternal grandparents. They were quiet, steady, sober New Englanders. My grandfather, as I mentioned, had been a baseball player. He had also been a fireman and policeman. After that began a long career as a minor functionary with the Elliott Addressing Machine Company. My grandmother, who in her younger days was a solo whistler on the church and lodge circuit, cooked, mended, busied herself about the house, and looked after me with untiring solicitude. The two played dominoes virtually every night of the years I lived with them. They encouraged me to study and to play. Athletic skills became a passion equalled only by my determination to make high grades in everything except conduct.

My grandparents, and various nearby relatives, were unenthusiastically associated with a neighborhood Congregational church of the conservative, evangelical type. Because God was quite a problem to me, I became the most ardent and faithful churchman of the family. The minister, a kind and careworn man whose preaching voice always sounded tearful, had officiated at my mother's funeral, and was keenly concerned about the state of my soul. The Sunday School superintendent, an austere, elderly dentist, believed in the literal fire of hell and was determined to guide me in another direction. From the beginning I was both a protégé and a problem child. Our relationship developed steadily but never smoothly.

In the sense that I was determined to ask "why" and "how do you know," I suppose my religious future was set the night my mother died, but it would be many years before I recognized it. If religion was to make sense to me, it had to provide room for my inquisitiveness and my rebellion. Somehow it had to encompass the anguish and bewilderment I felt at God's failure to save and preserve my mother. It had to be big enough to let me ask whether God was a demon, or whether God existed at all.

I expected to find answers in church, where the talk was interminably of God, Jesus, prayer and salvation. I listened and grew confused and impudent. I tried to pray. I listened hard for God's voice. I wanted to feel Jesus' arms about me. I prayed and had the increasingly embarrassed feeling that no one was listening. If God possessed a voice, it was strangely silent in my presence. The more I thought about the Jesus who was being revealed to me in my religious education, the more unappealing and unreal he became.

What my religious tutors failed to realize was that the spell of dissent was upon me like a divine discontent. It was not about meek acceptance and a cringing sense of sin that I wished to hear. I wanted to be challenged and shaken. I wanted my spirit to be given something to strive for. I wanted to know why the world could be at once such a wondrous and ugly place. I wanted to know why there was both laughter and hurt in me. If God created me, I wanted to know who created God. Instead, I was backed into a corner and implored to surrender my soul to the Lord and Savior.

I stayed with the neighborhood church until I went to college, and much of my social life was lived under its care. I knew from the time I was eleven or twelve years old that I could never be a Christian as the word was interpreted there, but I sang in the choir and rarely missed a Sunday evening Christian Endeavor meeting all through high school. These people were my friends, and though they trembled for my soul on grounds I considered nonsensical, I respected their sincerity and was grateful for their affection.

Such religion as I possess was born of conflict, and has been in its development a struggle *against* resentment as a wound inflicted upon me when I was unable to defend myself, and *for* a positive, constructive, unfettered spiritual freedom. In college there were added the dimensions of an awakened so-

cial conscience and a desire to commit my life to the direct
service of my fellow men. The open mind of classicism, the
probing mind of philosophy, the measuring mind of science,
and the eclectic mind of sociology impressed upon me the
endless diversity of man's spiritual searchings. A firm decision
against religious sectarianism was inevitable. I have sought
a spiritual life that offers not surrender and salvation but
"love of life in spite of life." I have striven to accept the
flaws and to find things to live for that transcend and conquer
them.

Faith, Admiration and Sympathy

For a time there was a genuine dilemma about a career.
My philosophical views were radically opposed to the structures of traditional theology, yet I felt a deep affection for
the church and looked upon it as a profoundly useful vehicle
for moral improvement and social progress. The ministry, it
seemed to me, was potentially one of the most rewarding
and constructive careers open to one whose mind responded
enthusiastically to religious questions, and who wanted, as I
did, to cultivate skills in education, in human relations, and
in the leadership of groups banded together to seek spiritual
fortification, idealistic encouragement and ethical effectiveness.

The passing years have only confirmed my early guess
about the ministry's possibilities. Mr. Mencken once described clergymen as ticket speculators outside the gates of
heaven. It is not uncommon, even now, for some intellectuals
to have a low regard for the clergy. In general, however, the
modern, well-trained and well-disciplined minister, priest or
rabbi holds an equal place in the intellectual firmament with
scientists, educators, poets and the like. He is respected as
a maker and transmitter of culture. He is regarded as a useful
and responsible community figure who, more often than not,
succeeds in practicing what he preaches.

Rather than being satirized, as by a Mencken or a Sinclair Lewis, the minister has instead become an object of intense solicitude. In the fifties there was a stream of sob stories about badgered, overworked, underpaid clergymen. One major magazine effort of this kind was entitled "Why Ministers Are Breaking Down." After enumerating a startling list of "brilliant" clerics who had been drained, exhausted and washed up at still tender ages, the article proceeded to analyze the minister's job as being like a horseman who is ordered to ride off in all directions at the same time. The blame was placed squarely on congregations for failing to understand and appreciate that impossible demands were being made of their spiritual leaders.

My own feeling, developed over the years, is that the "driven" clergyman is frequently the driver. That is, he drives himself for inner reasons he does not understand. The fact that many ministers *do* eventually wind up on a psychiatrist's couch is not an offense attributable merely to thoughtless congregations. In fact, it is not an offense at all. We are beginning to learn, in the selection and training of clergy, that an early psychiatric "vaccination" can fend off a lot of later heartaches and breakdowns. We understand very easily the necessity of a minister's warmth toward others, but we have been slower to realize how important it is for a clergyman to be able to warm up to himself: to like and respect himself enough to cherish, conserve and pace his own energies.

In the modern ministry, a man can fret himself into a breakdown. Few members of a congregation really know how easily he can work thirteen or fourteen hours a day, seven days a week, months at a time, if that is what he chooses to do. I say "chooses" though the choice may not necessarily be a conscious one. But the fact remains that a minister may, if he knows enough about himself, choose to live a relatively normal and balanced life of work and play, study and recreation, administration and recreation, activity and lethargy. In brief, a minister can learn to say no as well as yes. And I do not merely mean no to others. Equally I mean no to himself. One of the most important "yesses" a minister should learn to say to himself, incidentally, is, "Yes, I, also, am a man of flesh and not of stardust."

There are few professions in which there is not more work to be done than a person can ever hope to get done. The ministry decidedly shares this human plight, but the minister's task in coping with it is not essentially different from that in other responsible and burdened occupations.

No young man should go into the ministry unless he expects to work hard and still live with the frustrations of never getting his work wholly done. His ability to pace his life, space his energies, diversify his interests and enjoyments, is not something a congregation can do *for* him. It can do this *with* him, by making sensible and reasonable administrative arrangements and by assuming proper lay responsibilities, but first of all the minister must have the will and the ability to get off his own back. He must love and respect himself enough to want to be a whole person.

My feelings about the "underpaid" dirge are much the same. Unless the circumstances are unusual and compelling, a minister who is willing to be paid less than dignity requires is punishing himself for some inner entanglement he would do well to uncover and unravel. No man should enter the ministry expecting a salary equal to what he might earn in private industry, for that would be foolhardy. Unless his capabilities are such that he could command a greater income elsewhere, he shouldn't go into the ministry at all. But he should expect to be paid enough so that his wife and children are not unduly deprived by his yen for a full-time religious career. If a congregation is not sufficiently enthusiastic about what a competent minister is capable of offering to its individual and collective lives to pay him a respectable salary, the clergyman is doing no favor by becoming a suffering, threadbare servant. I speak now in terms of ordinary, present-day, American financial realities. There might well be special circumstances in which a minister would be willing to face starvation for the sake of a crucial cause or program. In that event we can assume that he would first make provision for the protection of his family.

Mr. Justice Brennan of the United States Supreme Court received a letter which read in part: "Would you use your influence to help my boy to become a Judge. He don't like hard work and I figure that sitting on a bench would suit him just fine."

If a man "don't like hard work," the ministry is no place for him. On the other hand, if a man isn't going to be able to learn to cherish himself enough to live broadly and variously, with due respect for his own limitations and needs, the ministry is no place for him either.

It is characteristic of a congregation to want at the helm a professional leader to whom the religious life is an all-pervasive, full-time, exacting occupation, making extraordinary claims upon intelligence and conscience. The minister, in other words, is an embodiment of spiritual specialization. This is not to say that laymen desire a minister to be ethereal and otherworldly. The evidence from surveys among Unitarian Universalist laity indicates unmistakably that while the preferred minister is scholarly, idealistic and sensitive, he is also, by overwhelming choice, earthy and pragmatic.

The key functions seem to be intensity and specialization. The layman senses that of necessity a layman's religion is a relatively cloistered thing. His preoccupations and distractions limit the scope of spiritual interest and cultivation. At first this sounds like a delirious reversal of terms. After all, it is generally assumed that if anyone lives in an ivory tower it is the clergyman. But it depends on what ivory tower we are talking about. If daily life, with its intricate web of demands and responses, is viewed as a confining cloister, then it *is* the layman's life that tends to be isolated from intimations and insights of spirit.

My years of association with laymen, of enjoying the privilege of knowing them inwardly as well as outwardly, convince me this is a truth etched and experienced deeply enough to be a congregation's basic motive for wanting a clergyman in its midst. Here is someone whose only reason for being, so far as his public and professional life is concerned, is to bring moral idealism to bear on every realm of human experience. Here is a person who, by the deliberate deed of a congregation, is given the time, the freedom and the sustenance to study, speak and act on the ethical and spiritual issues of living, and to help make more intelligible, to those who cannot claim such time and freedom, the religious resources available to them.

When a congregation experiences disappointment in its minister or, to be more concrete, when individual parishioners experience such disappointment, I am convinced that it is traceable mainly to a shattering of the image just described. If a minister fails, even unwittingly, to be the embodiment of the full-time religious life; if he fails, in some instance, to be the realization of a person who has the will and the courage to look at all aspects of life—political, personal, business, workaday, whatever—through the seeing eyes of religious insight and commitment, to that extent he is a disappointment to those who accept his ministry.

It makes me shudder to write these words, because they mean that every minister is destined to failure in his chosen life. No matter how much dedicated competence he achieves, he can never achieve enough. As Frederick May Eliot said —and he was easily one of the greatest of this century's Uni-

tarian ministers—"He [the minister] will preach his last sermon and make his last parish call with a sense of his own
ignorance and a prayer for forgiveness as he glances down
at his bungling hands."

Speaking now only of that ministry I really know, the
Unitarian Universalist, I feel that every man who enters it
chooses a labor at which he can never really succeed, because
its expectations always grow taller than its accomplishments.
Yet, for those who do choose it, there stretches out a life as
potentially satisfying and enriching as any this world offers.

Who is a Unitarian Universalist minister? He is a man,
never completely satisfied or satisfiable, never completely ad-
justed or adjustable, who walks in two worlds—one of things
as they are, the other of things as they ought to be—and loves
them both. He is a man with a pincushion soul and an elastic
heart, who sits with the happy and the sad in a chaotic pattern of laugh, cry, laugh, cry. And he knows deep down that
the first time his laughter is false, or his tears make-believe,
his days as a real minister are over.

He is a man with dreams he can never wholly share, partly
because he has some doubts about them himself and partly
because he is unable adequately to explain, describe, or define what it is he thinks he sees and understands.

A Unitarian Universalist minister is a man who continually runs out of time, out of wisdom, out of ability, out of
courage and out of money. He is hurtable. His tasks involve
great responsibility and little power. He must learn to accept
people where they are and go on from there. He must never
try to exercise influence he does not possess. If he is worth his
salt, he knows all this, and is still thankful every day of his
life for the privilege of being what he is.

The future of the liberal church is almost totally dependent on these two factors: great congregations (whether large
or small), and skilled, effective, dedicated ministers. The

strangest feature of their relationship is that they create one another.

It is generally assumed that churches go looking for people. I went looking for a church—the right church for me. I wanted to be a minister, but by the end of college the solution of where to minister was still not in sight. I took a job in industry and spent three valuable years learning what it means "to meet a payroll."

Consciousness of the possibilities in the Unitarian movement grew on me slowly. The merger of the two denominations was then only a dream. Gentle suggestions were made by some of my Quaker acquaintances, who were aware of my unresolved dilemma. As with so many I have met since, the real uniqueness of Unitarianism was unknown to me. My first, tentative visits to Unitarian churches were not inspiring. The intellectual calibre of the ministers seemed challenging enough, but I happened to hit places where the congregations were sparse, the atmosphere desultory, and the forms too traditional for my taste. But what I read of Unitarianism kept my curiosity alive, and one Sunday I found myself listening to John Haynes Holmes at New York's Community Church. The congregation was meeting in Town Hall, hardly an exalted setting, but John Haynes Holmes created a temple of the human spirit just by his being and his speaking. The congregation was vibrantly alive and was itself an eloquent symbol of human diversity. The service was religious—deeply religious—yet there were no divisive, mind-splitting, doctrinal elements.

During that hour I knew that if the Unitarian ministry was exciting enough to claim the talents of a John Haynes Holmes, it would have more than enough room in it for me. A door was open, and I wasted no time going through it. By the following summer I was enrolled in the Harvard Divinity School, with the warm encouragement and backing of the

American Unitarian Association. The opportunities to unfold, to grow in what Emerson called "faith, admiration and
sympathy" have never since ceased to amaze and inspire me.
I find what I need in this denomination and especially in the
congregations it has been my privilege to serve. Each in turn
has added memorable lessons to my life.

TWO

GETTING FROM SUNDAY TO MONDAY

*I say the whole earth and all the stars in the
sky are for religion's sake.
I say no man has ever yet been half devout enough,
None has ever yet adored or worship'd half enough ...*

WALT WHITMAN, *Starting from Paumanok*

WHEN we were building a new church edifice in Indianapolis, our six-year-old daughter raised the cry
that it didn't look like a church. "Why doesn't it have a
steeple?" she asked. When we reminded her that the old
building was also sans steeple, she still remained skeptical.
All the other churches in town had steeples or, at least,
towers.

Many of our churches *do* have steeples; in some cases,
magnificent ones. Our daughter was voicing the ageless pre-
disposition that churches should conform to a conventional
pattern. That pattern usually includes unquestioning belief
in a creed, submission to authority (of holy book, institution,
or hierarchy), and participation in prescribed rites and sacraments. To the uninitiated the most puzzling feature of Unitarian Universalist religion is its disregard of these ecclesiastical conformities.

There is an old anecdote about a group of Unitarians
who come to a fork in the road. On one road sign are the
words: "To Heaven." On the other: "To a Discussion about
Heaven." Without hesitation they choose their course. They

26

wouldn't think of missing a discussion! Like most legends, this one has its element of truth. A church is expected to require assent to certain concrete theological beliefs. Not so among Unitarian Universalists. Whether the subject is immortality, God or science, there may be as many ideas as there are people present, yet there will be one unifying principle; namely, the right of every person to make his own decision about what he believes. Hearing of this process for the first time, many are confused and puzzled. Others, coming suddenly upon it, fairly glow. "I've been a Unitarian Universalist for years without knowing it!" is an increasingly familiar refrain.

As a beginning, you might try some of these questions to see if they have an intimate ring:

I simply cannot accept religious beliefs on faith alone. Is there a church for me?

I believe in many things: man's essential dignity, human effort, the search for larger truths, the compelling need for ethical disciplines, the necessities of practical brotherhood; but I cannot bind my beliefs to a creedal test, nor place them beyond rational criticism. What church would want me?

In the end churches always seem to insist that religious truth is revealed and complete. Does any church welcome the idea that truth is an emerging, not a finished, thing?

Why shouldn't a child be encouraged to discover religion in his own unfolding life rather than have it laid upon him through a process of indoctrination? What church practices this?

Can any church be effective and still urge each member to be his free individual self?

There is self-evident beauty and truth in many of the world's historic religious faiths. Is there a church anywhere that welcomes and appreciates the insights and answers of all significant spiritual systems?

Where is the church that pays more than lip service to the fullest possible use of reason?

Can persons from many religious backgrounds— Christian, Jewish, Buddhist, Muslim, etc.—find one church where all are welcome without "conversion" or "renunciation"?

I want to be free to wonder about—even doubt—the existence of God, the nature of God, the effectiveness of prayer, the value of the Bible, the possibility of immortality, and still be religious. Where is the church that calls no honest doubt "heresy" and where heretics are welcome?

If you find a gleam of recognition in these questions, if they reflect some of your own thoughts, experiences and searchings, there is probably an exciting place for you in the Unitarian Universalist fold.

For us, the vital task in religion is to get from Sunday to Monday: to carry serious concern with religious living from the protected atmosphere of a worship service into the flesh and blood realities of daily living. Religions generally emphasize salvation, and most religions talk of salvation in terms of ceremonies, sacraments, catechisms and creeds. We speak warmly of salvation also, but in terms of *character*. We prefer to think of it as an achievement dependent on deeds rather than creeds.

"What must I do to be saved?" That was the question the jailer asked the Apostle Paul. His answer was a crucial one. It marked a point of no return for orthodox Christianity. Recall the full setting of this Biblical incident: In the city of Philippi, in the Roman colony of Macedonia, Paul and his associate, Silas, had been brought before the local magistrate for preaching religious doctrines frowned upon in the empire. After some manhandling by a mob, they were unceremoniously thrown into a prison cell where they immediately began praying and singing hymns. In the midst of this informal service a violent earthquake shook the cell door open and split the prisoners' chains.

The jailer, a sound sleeper who had evidently dozed through both the singing and the earthquake, thus proving himself to be a man of tolerably quiet conscience, awoke to find his prison doors swinging in the breeze. Panic-stricken at the certainty of his prisoners' escape, he drew his sword to commit suicide. In the nick of time, Paul cried out: "Do not harm yourself, for we are all here."

Overcome with gratitude, the jailer rushed toward Paul and Silas, pleading: "Men, what must I do to be saved?" And Paul replied: "Believe in the Lord Jesus, and you will be saved, you and your household."

Whenever I read this story I think of all the answers Paul might have given. He might even have asked a question of his own: "What do you mean 'saved'? Do you mean how can you live a decent, useful life, or do you mean how can you get to heaven?"

Paul simply assumed, as so many clergymen have gone on assuming ever since, that the jailer was only interested in getting his immortal soul into a celestial mansion. He further assumed that no desire could be dearer to the jailer's heart than to escape this nasty world. There was no consideration given to the possibility that life is an exceedingly precious gift, that it is a great privilege to be alive and to have chances to do something with a life. Nothing of that. Paul simply blurted out the formula. And not merely a formula but, from his point of view, *the* formula: "Believe in the Lord Jesus, and you will be saved, you and your household."

Here was the track of authoritarianism on which orthodox Christianity would run from Paul's day to our own. It did not occur to Paul that the jailer might have some thoughts and insights of his own worth probing and nurturing. Paul saw no reason whatever for encouraging the man to think, to use his own mind, to exercise his reason, to ponder the experiences of heart and conscience for satisfying religious answers. Paul said none of the words that might have moved Christianity in the direction of freedom and personal responsibility. Instead, he uttered a dogma. He said, in effect, this is not something to discuss, to weigh, to test by experience. No, this is something you simply accept.

Unitarian Universalists will have none of it. The kind of religion that commands our allegiance is the kind that respects our ability to make considered religious decisions of our own. We feel much more at home with the image of Jesus than with the image of Paul. The jailer asked a sincere question. He had been through an emotionally shattering experience. It made him think of ultimate things. "What must I do to be saved?" What a glorious opportunity for Paul to tell of Jesus' approach to the art of living. But not one word did he speak of the teachings of Jesus. All he had to offer was a theological doctrine; nothing about love, nothing about an aspiring morality, nothing about bold goodwill.

Compare this with a similar experience in the life of Jesus. It was a wealthy young man who came to Jesus with a question. "Rabbi," he asked, in more cultivated tones than Paul's jailer, "what must I do to inherit eternal life?" Jesus did not answer, "Believe on me and you will walk the golden streets." Instead he encouraged the young man to guide his life by the great ethical teachings of his religion. Forget about your wealth and bring riches instead into the lives of others!

The young man went away sorrowful, for he had great possessions. He wanted a formula. How much better he would have liked talking to Paul. Perhaps this is why orthodox Christianity became a religion *about* Jesus rather than a religion *of* Jesus. Yet, who knows what happened to the young man, when, in the privacy of his thoughts, he began to reflect on what the strange rabbi had told him?

For us, salvation is not an otherworldly journey, flown

on wings of dogma. It is ethical striving and moral achievement: respect for the personalities and convictions of others, faith in human dignity and potentiality, aversion to sanctimony and bigotry, hearty enjoyment of life and people, confidence in the true harmony of science and religion, faith in the ability to love, and a quest for broad, encompassing religious expression; spiritual yet practical, personal yet universal.

This is what we mean when we say we believe in salvation by character. Perhaps it would be more accurate to say that we believe salvation *is* character, for we do not mean that character saves a man from the flames of an imaginary hell or for the bliss of an equally imaginary heaven. We do not profess to know the precise dimensions of immortality. But we are sure of this: the inner life, shaped by the power of high and sane ideals, brings to the human soul the finest, most enduring satisfactions, and makes of a man a source of strength, even in the utmost tribulation, to the human family of which he is a member. This is what we mean by salvation, and what serves so well in life could not possibly serve less well in afterlife.

We believe that men are punished *by* their sins, not *for* them, and that the evil men do lives with them. By the same token, we believe that men are enriched by their virtues, and that the good they do lives with them as a benediction of peace in their own lives and in the life of humanity.

We believe that religion has no higher object than to teach us how to get from Sunday to Monday; how to take our Sunday professions into our Monday behavior, in short, when we talk of salvation, we talk of making religion a real force in our daily lives. We do not say that religion has nothing to do with the afterlife, but we do say that it has everything to do with this life.

THREE

BUT WHAT DO UNITARIAN
UNIVERSALISTS BELIEVE?

The world is my country,
All mankind are my brethren,
To do good is my religion,
I believe in one God and no more.

THOMAS PAINE

THE distinguished scholar and historian, Earl Morse
Wilbur, wrote: "To the Unitarian of today the marks
of true religion are spiritual freedom, enlightened reason,
broad and tolerant sympathy, upright character and unselfish
service."

Because we find the essence of religion in character and
conduct rather than in doctrines, creeds, dogmas and catechisms, those who normally think of religion as a series of
theological definitions find it frustrating to understand the
Unitarian Universalist position. We are believers, but our
beliefs are centered in a *method,* a process of the religious
life, rather than in closed articles of faith.

My telephone rings. The caller has read something in the
press that aroused curiosity. "Say, Reverend, I saw in the
paper where you didn't think it was such a hot idea for Billy
Graham to be coming to town."

"No, I didn't say that exactly. Read it again and you'll see
it was a little different."

"Oh, it doesn't matter too much, anyway, Reverend. I want to know what you Unitarians believe. I've never been to a Unitarian church. What's your creed?"

We have no creed. That's all there is to it. We have no creed! On matters normally frozen into creedal statements, a Unitarian Universalist is expected to follow the dictates of reason, conscience and experience. Our churches make no official pronouncements on God, the Bible, Jesus, immortality, or any of the other theological mysteries generally answered with unabashed finality by the more traditional religious groups.

By its very nature, a creed is final, complete and binding on all professedly religious people. It is held to be above reasonable examination. Its divine origin is assumed. Actually, if the historic church creeds were divinely revealed, they came into being in a strangely human manner. There were more than two centuries of speculation, debate and bitter strife before the first "final" Christian creed, the Nicene, gained acceptance. It and its companion piece, the Apostles', cannot possibly be viewed historically as anything but compromises, based on an accommodation of conflicting views.

The traditional creeds are human products, and they were probably the best possible expressions of Christian belief in the third and fourth centuries. What we cannot accept is that these creeds should be binding on this and future generations. To us, creating a religious way of life is far too important to be left to the distant past's propounders of doctrine. We are Unitarian Universalists, not by substituting one confession of faith for another, but by opening our minds to receive truth and inspiration from every possible source— even from the ancient creeds, if by critical examination they throw genuine light on current concerns.

The most fundamental of all Unitarian Universalist principles, then, is *individual freedom of religious belief*—the principle of the free mind.

Most religious beliefs are based on outside authority. The prophet or priest dictates, the Holy Book dictates, or the creed dictates what must be believed. For those who have no special urge to do their own thinking, this is an effective and logical approach. I was once reproached by a man of impressive intellectual gifts and scientific achievements. He told me that I was doing a great disservice by exhorting people to try to think out their own religious answers. "Religion is a specialty," he said. "It should be left to experts."

Unitarian Universalists are people who cannot leave their religious beliefs in the care of "experts." For us, the most vital faith about man is this: in order to advance, he must be free. There is no area of life in which it is more important for him to be free than in the realm of spirit.

Those who differ with us argue that man must be directed by infallible religious guides, or his inherent frailties will corrupt and destroy him. But when we begin to examine closely the "infallible" religious guides, what do we discover? The church which claims authority to dictate beliefs is a human institution, and its "final truths" are no more than the conclusions arrived at by earlier human leaders.

The same statement is true of the Bible. It was written by mortal men.

No creed exists that was not originally hammered out under pressure by human beings like ourselves.

Churches, Bibles and creeds are the creations of men who once exercised their freedom to create. Is there any reason why we should expect to do less? We accept the birth of a new age in all kinds of human enterprises, why not in religion also? Atoms and space satellites are symbols of a revolution in concepts of truth and reality. The traditions and habits on which the religions of past millennia were founded are limping. Either we go forward with religious sentiments and formulations adequate to our time, or time will go forward and leave us cringing in the ancient caves of our spiritual forefathers.

The distinctive characteristic of the religious liberal is his insistence that he will not bind his present and future in religion to the tutelage of the past. He will attempt to learn all that the past can teach him, *but he will do his own thinking about current matters of faith and belief.*

In the words of John P. Marquand, Pulitzer Prize author: "As Democracy is man's freest form of social life so is Unitarianism the freest religious life, and like Democracy, the Unitarian religion depends upon the separate thinking of every Unitarian to give it significance and vitality."

In a Unitarian Universalist congregation an agnostic may sit beside one who believes in a personal God; at the after-service coffee hour a believer in personal immortality may stand chatting with one who accepts "utter extinction." Such are our wide diversities of individual belief.

We are *together* in our devotion to spiritual freedom; each living by a considered, examined, thought-out covenant with himself and with life as a whole; each understanding, even hoping, that his beliefs may change as insights deepen and life's lessons grow.

Earthly and Practical Reason

Second only to the free mind is our belief in *reason* and *responsibility.* Freedom requires responsibility, and responsibility requires reason. Man must accept responsibility for his acts. We believe that this sense of responsibility reflects the teachings of the great Biblical prophets, from Amos to Jesus. We believe also that it is the essence of one of man's noblest achievements, the scientific method. In brief, we believe that our religious concept of ethical responsibility is much more in tune with reality, and much more productive of good, than the traditional doctrine of man's inherent depravity through "original sin."

"Why am I such a failure?" she said. The woman sitting in my study looked like anything but a failure. She and her husband were my good friends. I had been in their home many times. It was a tasteful and orderly household. The three children were healthy and bright. There were no unusual financial problems, and the marriage was sound. Yet this woman was struggling with an insidious sense of guilt and inadequacy. A "tradition of inferiority" was poisoning her life.

Where does this tradition come from? Why are people so conscious of their failings and limitations that they are literally unable to think of good things as flowing from their lives? One of the most widespread causes, in my opinion, is the doctrine of sin, stressed in early religious training and magnified until it comes to be regarded, deep in the recesses of personality, as inherent, innate evil from which there is no real escape.

Nothing is more appalling to me than the crippling effects of those religions which fill the individual with consciousness of his hopeless condition, his wicked and disgraceful alienation from goodness and virtue. Each person's experience contains enough emotional conflict, enough regret, enough self-reproach to give force to the doctrines of original sin and total depravity. The eloquently remorseful outcry of the Apostle Paul vividly expressed our conflicts of habit and aspiration: "For the good that I would, I do not: but the evil which I would not, that I do. O wretched man that I am! who shall deliver me from the body of this death?"

With such a ghastly portrait of human nature, sharply contrasted with the perfection and beauty of the divine life, how could one avoid the conclusion that the sources of the good life are nowhere to be found within man himself? But a realistic study of human nature reveals a plethora of impulses and a rich diversity of motives within which the process of moral selection proceeds. We find some things to be better, and some things to be worse, by the method of trial and error, by measurements of happiness and welfare, by comparison and reflection. *This is how man actually cultivates responsible behavior!* For Unitarian Universalists a chief resource to this end is *human reason*. With us reason holds the place that is ordinarily accorded to revelation in orthodox religions! That person is likely to behave best who exercises his reason most.

This does not mean that we are unmindful of the limitations of human reason, nor that we look upon it as an infallible guide. In our way of life there are *no* infallible guides. One of the most gifted of Unitarian ministers, Dr. E. Burdette Backus, has described our faith in reason in this manner: "... the intelligence of man is an instrument which has developed in the process of his evolution to enable him to satisfy his needs more adequately. It had originally a very earthy and practical purpose, namely that of solving the problems that pressed in upon him in daily life. Although it continues this immediately pressing function, it has far outsoared it and seeks to penetrate beyond the stars to find an answer to the riddle of the universe. Our reason makes many mistakes; it is frequently taken captive by our desires, so that we believe things not because they are true but because we want to believe them. It cannot give us absolute and final certainty, but it has established a substantial body of verified truth; it is steadily increasing the amount of that truth. For all its limitations it serves us very well, and those who advocate its abandonment are simply telling a man who is groping his way through the dark by the light of a candle to blow out the light."

Unitarian Universalism, then, is an ethical rather than a doctrinal religion, with individual freedom as its method and with reason as its guide. It should not be assumed, however, that we practice reason in an austere and overly solemn manner. When we succeed in seizing upon the finer and more elevating aspects of experience, projecting them enlarged and colorfully enhanced upon the canvasses of life, they become the source of the warmest joy and blessedness. Our purpose is to enable heart and mind to capture realizations of what life can be when men live up to their best. Through expanded imagination, awakened conscience and enriched beauty there springs a spiritual fellowship whose inspiration to deeper satisfaction and more ample living has a force greater than all other experiences of life.

The path of the liberal religious journey leads from freedom, through reason, to a third fundamental principle: *a generous and tolerant understanding of differing views and practices.*

Unity with Diversity

Churches are social institutions, sometimes sociable, sometimes not. They have a curious double function. They are at once the cause and effect of the interests they represent. This is not unusual. Happy homes are the outgrowth of mutual love and they are producers of affectionate personalities. Schools are products of concern for knowledge and they inspire love of learning in those who attend them. Churches are created by religious interest and zeal, and the activities of church life awaken and deepen the spiritual aspirations of those who participate. If only the first part of this function is emphasized, it encourages some to proclaim that churches are not necessary to the religious life—"I can get all the religion I need working in my garden." When only the second part is stressed, it tempts some to conclude that churches are the sole sources of religion. Each view is fragmentary and one-sided. All institutions are at the same time the yield and source of the convictions they embody. Concern for the care of the emotionally-disturbed draws people together into Mental Health Associations, and in turn the Associations stimulate the improvement of individual mental hygiene and hospital care. Love of the spiritual life draws religionists together; organized religion encourages the further quest for religious guidance and understanding.

Most churches find their bond of union in scriptural or creedal affirmations. Acceptance into membership is based on uniformity of professed theological belief, usually accompanied by some required rite or rites. We believe that people can work together for the betterment of character, the advancement of spiritual life, and the improvement of society without conforming to a set pattern of theological doctrines. In fact, we go well beyond this to express our conviction that differing theological views are natural and healthy and that attempts to enforce religious conformity are deadening and potentially destructive. History is witness to the horrors of religious intolerance.

We hold that churches are voluntary associations of individuals for fostering the highest forms of life they can fathom. In churches, people join to inspire themselves, their children, and the human community; to discover and give their loyal effort to ideal manners of living. The atmosphere of a Unitarian Universalist church encourages each person to make his best contribution to the group's enrichment. The emphasis is on sharing the results of personal thought and evaluation. Truth, we recognize, is vast and many-sided. Why should we all have the same theology? It is a basic part of our faith that people of widely differing religious backgrounds and views can work cheerfully and productively under the same church roof, strengthening each other for the great tasks of making human life more splendid, more precious and more secure. This attitude is the eminently practical one of measuring religion by its contributions to the character and well-being of those who cherish it. By making this conception explicit in the organized life of the church, we unfurl the standards of truth and value within experience itself, and make them subject to the judgment and conscience of the people who actually constitute the body of the institution.

When a conscientious seeker asks what we believe, he must make an effort to lay aside the theological definitions employed to describe most churches. Ours is very definitely a *different kind* of church, and it requires a different kind of definition. Yet, let there be no mistake about the fact that the Unitarian Universalist fellowship is a purposeful, positive, *organized* religious movement, dedicated to the moral, aesthetic, philosophical, scientific and social progress of human life. It welcomes all who catch the vision of placing principles of freedom, responsibility, reason and tolerance above uniform theological doctrines. Our churches are free associations of individuals, striving by every honest means to nurture the highest forms of life that experience and imagination can devise. We are bound by no historic model or established set of dogmas. We continue to evolve in the light of our growing knowledge of ourselves and our world. We feel obliged by the very urgency of religion to seek and experiment with more effective forms of teaching our members, young and old, with more compelling and inspiring symbols in all the arts, with more energetic and adequate methods of public service, and with more moving and sustaining sources of comfort and courage in the high adventure of reasonable and idealistic living.

FOUR

HOW DID WE GET THIS WAY?

Say, why was man so eminently raised
Amid vast creation? why ordained
Through life and death to dart his piercing eye,
With thoughts beyond the limit of his frame?

MARK AKENSIDE, *The Pleasures of Imagination*

THE plane on which I traveled landed at the Athens air-
port in the eerie half-light of dawn. By the time the
customs formalities were over, the rising edges of the sun
had placed a halo over the nearby hills. A taxi took me
swiftly along the Pireus, and headed up a broad avenue toward the city's heart. Suddenly, it was in sight! The Acrop-
olis, silhouetted against the brilliant morning sky! It was one
of the most moving experiences of my life. In a strange land,
I was coming home—home to the Socratic, Athenian cradle
of my Unitarian Universalist religion.

"Do you then be reasonable," said delightful Socrates to
Crito, "and do not mind whether the teachers of philosophy
are good or bad, but think only of Philosophy herself. Try
to examine her well and truly; and if she be evil, seek to
turn away all men from her; but if she be what I believe she
is, then follow her and serve her, and be of good cheer."
With such words were laid the foundations of the free human
spirit, the examined life, and the endless quest for elusive
truth and incomparably glorious knowledge. Liberal religion was planted in ancient Athens.

41

On another trip it was my good fortune to spend an hour in Israel with the great Jewish philosopher and theologian, Martin Buber. He is a gnomelike man, barely five feet tall, with a huge head and a magnificent, flowing white beard. His eyes are large, brown, and compassionate. His study, in a shaded, one-story, stucco house in Jerusalem, deserves the skill of a Dickens for proper description: Victorian desk and divan, a lamp that must have been designed immediately after Edison's invention of the electric bulb, random heaps of books, brochures, pamphlets and manuscripts.

During the early part of our interview, I scribbled notes furiously. Suddenly there was silence, and when I looked up into Buber's face, he was smiling. "Mr. Mendelsohn," he said, "either you can take notes without really listening, or you can really listen without taking notes."

It was said without a trace of harshness. I firmly closed the notebook and "really listened" as he said: "Throughout the world, there is a spiritual front on which is being waged a secret, silent struggle between the desire to be on life's side and the desire to destroy. This is the most important front of all—more important than any military, political or economic front. It is the front on which *souls are moulded.*"

My next question was the obvious one: "What can an individual do to tip the balance?"

Buber gazed out the window for a moment; then he turned toward me and said: "No one can chart a day by day course of action for anyone else. Life can only be determined by each situation as it arises. Every person has his chance. From the time he gets up in the morning until the time he retires at night he has meetings with others. Sometimes he even meets himself! He sees his family at breakfast. He goes to work with others. He meets people in the streets. He attends gatherings with others. Always there are others. What he does with each of these meetings is what counts.

The future is determined more by this than by ideologies and proclamations."

In sitting with Buber I felt that I was in the presence of another remarkable Hebrew prophet—one whose lineage extended directly back to Amos, Hosea, Isaiah, Jeremiah, and Jesus. I was moved, as in Athens, by a sense of coming home, in still another strange land, to the roots of my Unitarian Universalist religion.

Modern liberal religion heartily acknowledges its debt to these two founts of reverence for the dignity of man and the primacy of ethics in religion: Athens and Israel.

The Christian origins of our movement are anchored in the moral teachings of Jesus, as exemplified in the Beatitudes and the Sermon on the Mount. We realize, however, that there are many complications in making an "historical" assessment of Jesus. Most of us believe that on the basis of the evidence available to us, Jesus, at most, thought of himself as the Jewish Messiah. It was later followers and interpreters, like the Apostle Paul, who transformed Jesus into a Christian Savior atoning to God for the sins of mankind.

In a technical sense, early Christianity was neither Trinitarian nor Unitarian. For nearly three centuries after Jesus' death no specific doctrine of this type was enforced as part of an official Christian creed. When doctrinal controversies became overly stormy and violent, the Roman emperor Constantine summoned church leaders to a council at Nicaea where, in A.D. 325—almost three hundred years after the death of Jesus—the Nicene Creed was voted into existence. The deity of Jesus thus became the official orthodoxy of Christian religion. The Nicene formula declared, by a divided vote, that Jesus was of the *same essential substance* as God. It is characteristic of Unitarian Universalists to doubt the validity of this decision and to emphasize instead the *human* characteristics of Jesus.

A half-century later, at another gathering of church leaders

—the General Council of Constantinople—the assembled dignitaries added the Holy Spirit to their formula, thus completing the Trinity. I have oversimplified the history, but essentially this was the very human manner in which the Trinitarian dogma of "Father, Son and Holy Spirit" came into existence. From the beginning there were sincere and thoughtful Christians who felt that the moral message of Jesus was being lost in a sea of metaphysics, but it quickly became apparent that those who could not conscientiously accept the Trinitarian position were to be expelled, condemned, and perhaps martyred as heretics.

It is worth noting that the only early sources we have of the actual teachings of Jesus and his immediate disciples are the first three Gospels. In their present form, these were probably written from one to two generations after Jesus' death. There is not the remotest suggestion of the Trinitarian formula in them. Indeed, Jesus—or any other Jew of his age—would have been shocked by the "blasphemy" of such a conception.

Earl Morse Wilbur in *Our Unitarian Heritage* says:

"... during long centuries of their national humiliation no other conviction had been so deeply burned into the consciousness of the Jewish people as their belief in the absolute and unqualified oneness of God. In fact, down to this very day, nothing else has proved such an impassable barrier to the reception of Christianity by the Jews, as has the doctrine of the Trinity, which has seemed to them to undermine the very cornerstone of their religion." *

It is a minor but interesting facet of Christian history that as late as the fifth century, in an enclave east of the Jordan, a lonely handful of Jewish Christians, known as Ebionites, clung to their original beliefs in the unity of God and the pure humanity and natural birth of Jesus.

From the time of Jesus to the Council of Chalcedon, a

* Beacon Press, p. 9.

period of roughly four hundred and fifty years, orthodox Christian doctrine, against which European Unitarianism and Universalism were eventually to protest, emerged with the belief that *God, while one, exists in three persons, and that one of these persons (Jesus) has two natures (divine and human).*

It is all too easy for the modern religious freethinker to look back on the controversies which shook the early Christian Church and conclude that centuries were spent in nonsensical strife over the words rather than over vital matters of the spiritual life. From Nicaea to Chalcedon, the councils seem to have labored mightily to bring forth verbal formulas that twirl in meaningless circles. It must not be overlooked, however, that to Christian believers of the third and fourth centuries the very essence, and perhaps even the existence, of their faith, hung on their finding solutions to the questions at issue. In fairness it must be granted that the struggles represented deep religious perplexities of the time.

Earl Morse Wilbur has written: "The character and methods of the Councils that established these doctrines are not, it is true, calculated to give us great reverence for their Christian character, nor much respect for their opinions; while the repeated interference of the civil power to enforce decisions of doctrine in its own interest was as vicious as it well could be. Yet the changes of thought . . . do not quite deserve to be called, as they often have been, 'corruptions of Christianity.' No one tried, or wished, to 'corrupt' the Christian faith. It was, indeed, a vast change from the simple religion of the sermon on the mount and the parables of Jesus to the theology of the Nicene and Athanasian Creeds; and the whole emphasis shifted from a religion of the heart and life to abstract speculations of the head. Yet when we have made all deductions for the political intrigues and the mean jealousies and the unscrupulous ambitions that so often accompanied them, we find at the bottom of these controversies an earnest and honest desire in the best minds to state the theory of the new Christian religion in terms which the cultured old world of Greek thought could accept." *

Anyone who has ever struggled for a cause can appreciate the fervor which attached to the doctrines of the Trinity and the deity of Jesus. For early Christians their emergence was the result of a life and death exertion. Once achieved, they *must* be defended as the essence of Christian faith. Whoever disavowed or contradicted them seemed to endanger the very soul of Christianity. It is always a temptation to identify orthodoxy with religion itself. Christians fell victim to the temptation. They came to look upon heresy as the most vicious and contemptible of crimes. Centuries later, when a few brave and enterprising spirits began to compare the Creeds with the New Testament and concluded that they preferred a belief in God's unity and Jesus' humanity to the enigmas of the Trinity and the God-Man, they were attacked with a fanaticism that considered the most extreme punishment to be no more than what these "enemies of religion" justly deserved.

Thus, through all the early history of liberal religion there is a strain of violent persecution. Tragedy and death stalked those who first laid the foundations in Europe of the movement that was to bear the Unitarian name. And it was not only the Trinity and the God-Man which were to come under critical scrutiny. Other zealously guarded doctrines were also questioned. First to be questioned was Augustine's doctrine, later elaborated by Calvin, that the nature of man, even in infancy, is totally corrupted by sin. Next, another of Augustine's theological doctrines—also stressed by Calvin—that God had decided at the very beginning which souls to save and which to consign to eternal damnation was denied. Finally, the notion of "vicarious

---

* *Our Unitarian Heritage*, Beacon Press, pp. 32-33.

atonement"—that Jesus provided salvation by paying for the sins of mankind—was examined and discarded.

Thus the forerunners of Unitarianism struck not only at the two central doctrines of orthodox Christianity, but at three lesser ones as well. From the beginning they staked the merit of their argument on the plea that the five dogmas were inconsistent with Scripture and offensive to reason and the moral sense.

Nothing that could properly be called a Unitarian or Universalist movement came into existence until the Protestant Reformation was in full flow, but this does not mean that there were no liberal pioneers prior to the sixteenth century.

Each creative age produces unusually creative individuals. Such a one was Origen, born in Alexandria in A.D. 185, who was the most productive writer and the most liberal thinker in the first millennium of Christian history. His was the least dogmatic and most rationalistic interpretation of Christianity to appear prior to the time of Erasmus, and richly deserves recognition as a pioneer of the tradition that would one day give birth to liberal religion. Soundly schooled in science, philosophy and theology, he insisted that faith and knowledge were not antagonistic, and that religion was not endangered by the rational search for truth. Absent from his makeup was the bigotry of the narrower-minded Christians who did their best to suppress the rich spiritual heritage of Greek and Stoic philosophy. He believed that the Bible was something to be studied critically as well as reverently, and he denied that it was necessary to accept the Bible literally in all instances.

A biographer, Fred G. Bratton, writes: "From the standpoint of charm and versatility, Origen is one of the most appealing characters in history. His independence of mind prejudiced orthodoxy against him so that he was never beatified, but not all saints are canonized. Owing to his comparatively liberal views, the historic Christian Church has never given him his rightful place either as a thinker or as a Christian character." *

What were some of his "comparatively liberal views"? He was the first scientific theologian. What mattered to Origen was not the confirmation of orthodox doctrines, but the fullest possible application of reason, tolerance and cultural adjustment to the problems of the religious life. As with Spinoza, he was inclined to reject anything that was unreconcilable with reason. Where Tertullian exclaimed: "I believe it because it is absurd," and Augustine insisted: "I would not believe the Gospel if the authority of the Catholic Church did not compel me," Origen consistently promoted rationality as the basis of belief.

He was a forerunner of Luther in upholding faith as the soul of religion, but he led where Luther did not follow in proclaiming that faith is worthless unless it expresses itself in ethical conduct. Throughout his writings it is the ethical emphasis, as well as the glorification of reason, that stamp him as a fountainhead of the liberal tradition. By renouncing dogma, by disclaiming prejudice and ignorance, by respecting the insights of the Classical as well as the Christian world, by celebrating reason, and by upholding the ethical imperatives of faith, Origen richly deserves a primary place in our affection.

Another early figure of genuine significance was the British monk, Pelagius, whose lifetime extended roughly from A.D. 360-420. His major contribution was a courageous advocacy of free will and individual freedom at a time when the monumental intelligence of Augustine and his insistence on the total depravity of human nature dominated the Christian scene. Pelagius, like Origen, preached an ethical religion. Because he was himself a man of impressive learning and undeniably honorable character, Augustine looked upon him as an exceedingly dangerous threat to orthodoxy.

* *The Legacy of the Liberal Spirit*, Scribner's, pp. 8-9.

The two engaged in what must have been the "Lincoln-Douglas" debates of their time. "If I ought, I can," argued Pelagius. "God created man upright, but man, having of his own free will become depraved and having been justly condemned, begat a posterity in the same state of depravation and condemnation," answered Augustine.

Dean Inge once said: "A religion succeeds, not because it is true, but because it suits its worshipers." There can be no doubt that the Christians of the fifth century overwhelmingly favored Augustine's enthusiasm for human damnation. The faithful repudiated Pelagius along with his confidence in their moral competence. One consequence was the adoption of Cyprian's doctrine that in view of human depravity there could be no salvation outside the Church. Christians would wait a long time for a reassertion of the universalistic, rational, and encouraging faith of Pelagius that sin is "a thing of will and not of nature."

I like to think of Origen and Pelagius as bridges by which Greek rationality and Hebrew ethical religion made their way across the stream of Christian orthodoxy into the developing liberal religion of the modern world. Perhaps there would have been others if they had never lived, and, in fact, there were others, though of lesser force, who would nurture the seeds of reason and moral freedom, keeping them alive for the day when the climate would change and they would burst forth to challenge orthodoxy. I like to think of Origen and Pelagius as having won great though, for a long time, hidden victories for the free human spirit. I fear that most Unitarian Universalists are unaware of the surpassing debt owed by religious liberals to these two uncanonized saints of the Catholic Church.

With the ferment of the Protestant Reformation, many adventurous opportunities were opened for the more liberal religious mind. Sister to the Reformation was the Renaissance, spelling the downfall of medievalism and laying the

foundations of the modern outlook. Revolutionary theories
of the universe shattered Biblical cosmology, questioned Aris-
totelian logic, and undermined medieval supernaturalism.

The tiny sailing ships of Columbus, Magellan and de
Gama, proved the earth's roundness by refusing to fall off the
edge of the ocean. World trade was shifted from the Adriatic
to the Atlantic, and men's minds were stretched to new geographical frontiers.

Great centers of art and philosophy were created in Flor-
ence, Rome, Augsburg. Genius was encouraged and nurtured. Man was celebrated; individualism honored; freedom
praised. A new trust in human nature rose. Science and the
life of reason grew in luxuriant revolt against absolutism
and authoritarianism.

In *The Legacy of the Liberal Spirit*,* Fred G. Bratton
calls our attention to the fact that all too little is made by
biographers of Leonardo da Vinci's prophetic spirit as a
religious philosopher. His artistic and scientific genius is
amply recognized, but he was equally impressive as an independent thinker in religion. Once again we encounter a
generally unheralded precursor of modern liberal religion.
Deeply committed to religion as an ethical rather than a
mystical imperative, Leonardo was an avowed critic of cleri-
calism, fanaticism, superstition, and dogma. He spoke with
candid disapproval, long before Erasmus or Luther, of the
worship of Mary and the saints, the sale of indulgences, and
confession. He made no secret of his scorn for astrology,
witchcraft and alchemy.

He fully recognized the implications of the philosophical
conflict between freedom and authority, and he was a solid
partisan of freedom. He wrote: "When besieged by ambi-
tious tyrants, I find the means of defense in order to preserve
the chief gift of nature which is liberty." Impatient with the

* Scribner's, pp. 62-64.

church-controlled scientists of his time, and perhaps smarting under the ban imposed by the Church on his anatomical studies, Leonardo wrote: "Those sciences are vain and full of errors which are not born of experience, mother of all certitude, and which do not terminate in observation. . . . I will make experiment before I proceed because my intention is first to set forth the facts and then to demonstrate the reason why such experience is constrained to work in such fashion. And this is the rule to be followed by the investigators of natural phenomena: while nature begins from causes and ends with experience, we must follow a contrary procedure, that is, begin from experience and with that discover the causes."

Leonardo was Greece reborn, the Renaissance incarnate, the liberal mind come to being! It was the Renaissance as well as the Reformation that pointed ahead to our religious philosophy.

Luther and Calvin exchanged the Pope for the Bible, but left undisturbed the Latin theology of orthodox Christian religion. They altered the techniques for attaining salvation, and by making Scripture rather than the Holy See the ultimate source of spiritual authority, they guaranteed a multiplicity of rival sects in the Christian world. They did not, except by indirection, encourage the life of reason in religion or the cultivation of trust in human nature. They did, however, assert the individual priesthood of all believers, and by so doing opened the gates to those who would establish the footings of the Unitarian and Universalist edifices.

Fourteen years after Martin Luther nailed his ninety-five theses to the Wittenberg Castle Church door, Michael Servetus startled the Christian world with a furiously written book entitled *On the Errors of the Trinity*. It was a bold, angry denunciation of the dogma of the Trinity as upheld by both Reformation and Catholic theologians. The most widely quoted of Servetus' phrases is the one which reads: "Your

Trinity is the product of subtlety and madness. The Gospel knows nothing of it."

The author of these heretical sentences was nineteen years of age. His style was chaotic and intemperate, but it demonstrated a phenomenal range of reading. The book was placed on sale in the Rhine cities, and spread rapidly through Switzerland, Germany and northern Italy. Perhaps because of his youth, Servetus believed for a time that the major reformers would embrace his arguments as soon as they could consider them. Luther quickly put an end to such hope when he labeled the book "abominably wicked." Condemnation assumed epic proportions.

Servetus responded by asking to write a second book in which he would attempt to correct the mistakes of the first. At Basel he was given indulgence to do so. The result was a smaller volume called *Dialogues on the Trinity*. He left out some of the objectionable passages of his earlier effort, and tried to express himself in language more nearly like that of recognized Church teachers. In the end, however, he restated the same thoughts as before. Rather than mollifying his critics, he shocked them more than ever. Lacking both friends and money, he disappeared from sight for more than twenty years.

Nearly a quarter of a century later, when he was on trial for his life, the books on the Trinity had been so hotly suppressed one could not be found for use in the court.

What terrible teachings did these volumes contain? Servetus claimed that God cannot be divided and that no such doctrine is taught in the Bible. Creedal terms like Trinity, essence, and substance, he said, are inventions and foreign to Scripture. The Trinity and the doctrine of two natures in Christ actually keep men from being true Christians. They are illogical, unreasonable, contradictory, and imaginary. They raise unanswerable questions, lead to countless heresies, and leave men, in effect, with no God at all. Moreover they are a barrier to the conversion of Jews and Moslems, and are therefore obstacles to the spread of Christianity. The progress of religion requires the uprooting of these doctrines.

The ultimate end of Michael Servetus was martyrdom. Calvin had him burned at the stake after he had enlarged his earlier books into a major work.

The Unitarian Movement

It is a mistake to call Servetus a Unitarian. His system was his own and attracted no school of followers. His contribution was to launch others on lines of thought which led in time to modern liberal religion. The orthodox Protestant reformers fastened upon the Trinity with vehemence, while more and more men arose who challenged it and other theological doctrines. Equally significant was the sharpness with which the issue of the right to heresy was drawn. The drama of Servetus raised searching questions about the cruelty of religious intolerance. Castellio spoke for growing numbers when he wrote: ". . . to burn a man alive does not defend a doctrine, but slays a man."

Almost as if in response to Castellio's eloquence, movements developed in Poland and Transylvania, which were the real beginnings of European Unitarianism. In theology they were un-Trinitarian. Of greater consequence was their devotion to the principles of freedom, rationality and tolerance in religion. The movement in Poland was headed by the saintly Faustus Socinus. He organized liberal congregations, persuaded them to give up extreme positions, and defended them in their controversies with both Catholic and Protestant opponents. The movement spread rapidly, attracting many of the most advanced, cultivated and talented of Poles. In spite of later persecution, a lasting impression was left on the history of Polish culture. Church records were eventually destroyed, but it is generally believed that by

1618 there were more than three hundred Socinian congregations.

Persecution mounted, under Jesuit leadership, until it became an uncompromising war of extermination. To the very end of their existence the Socinians carried on an active program of education at home and abroad. They were bold and aggressive, but depended far more on reason and discussion than on passion or eloquence. They tried to set an example of good temper and mild speech in religious argument, and won many converts by their efforts. In the end they were overwhelmed by a flood of persecution. Their high moral standards were no defense against the determination to root out every vestige of their heresies. Socinus himself was attacked in the streets of Krakow. By order of a Polish knight, his face was smeared and his mouth filled with mud. This was the beginning of a series of personal attacks that left him a broken man.

The policy of extermination assumed systematic proportions, and the Socinian movement was utterly destroyed in Poland. Exiles scattered over the face of Europe in one of the most tragic and plaintive chapters in the history of religious persecution. A few found their way to a haven in Transylvania where, for some time, there had been well-organized churches of their own type and outlook. Under the leadership of the brilliant Francis David, Transylvania had become the scene of an energetic movement actually bearing the name Unitarian. It is worth noting that the label was not chosen by Francis David's followers but was bestowed, as a term of condemnation, by orthodox critics. The Transylvanian liberals stressed the humanness of Jesus. They were considered to be enemies of the Trinity—thus Unitarians. By the late sixteenth century, there were more than four hundred such-labelel congregations in the surrounding area.

At the peak of his career, Frances David was Transylvania's outstanding religious figure and one of Europe's ablest preachers and theologians. Under his guidance, the only Unitarian king in history, John Sigismund of Transylvania, issued the western world's first edict of religious freedom and toleration. It read in part: ". . . preachers shall be allowed to preach the Gospel everywhere, each according to his own understanding of it. If the community wish to accept such preaching, well and good; if not, they shall not be compelled, but shall be allowed to keep the preachers they prefer. No one shall be made to suffer on account of his religion, since faith is the gift of God."

This Bill of Rights in religion marks a precious moment in Unitarian history, for it kept liberal religious faith from being destroyed as it was in Poland and elsewhere. This is not to say that the Transylvanian Unitarians escaped persecution. John Sigismund's successors were persuaded to adopt anti-Unitarian policies. By 1574, David's life and teachings were under hostile scrutiny and within a year many of his most noted followers were being executed, mutilated, or deprived of their rights and property. By 1579, David himself was thrown into prison, and allowed to die of exposure and neglect. Nevertheless, the spirit of religious liberty, preached by David and promulgated by John Sigismund, was never completely crushed. The Unitarian churches of Transylvania persist to this day. Now a part of Communist Rumania, they once again need the full force of David's inspiring example of unswerving loyalty to his faith.

Francis David, in his beliefs and teachings, never shrank from taking the next step in his chosen task of carrying out a consistent reformation of Christianity. This placed him far in advance of the more cautious Socinus. It also propelled him ahead of his time by a wide margin. Of the earlier Unitarian leaders, he alone would probably feel at home among contemporary religious liberals.

The Unitarians and Universalists effected a complete merger in Boston in May, 1960, after many years of strengthening ties. Created by the same historical forces, the two movements that came together at that time were the results of similar but separate beginnings. Since my introduction to the denomination was through Unitarianism, its story is the more familiar to me. Let us trace its modern course separately, returning eventually to the parallel account of Universalism.

The story of Unitarian pioneering in England is happier than on the Continent. While it is true that the first stages of the Reformation were marked by occasional executions and frequent imprisonments, there was a steady movement toward toleration of heresy in England. Long before Unitarians attempted to organize themselves, capital punishment and imprisonment for dissident religious beliefs had been banished from the English landscape. There were civil persecutions, to be sure, but the stake, gallows, and prison bars were no longer obstacles to the development of religious thought.

Socinianism exercised influence among progressive English religious thinkers well into the eighteenth century. Early English Unitarians acknowledged their debt to the Polish movement by applying three principles: they advocated Socinian tolerance of difference in belief, they used the Socinian test of reason for religious doctrines, and they preached the Socinian concepts of God, Jesus, and the atonement.

England's developing Unitarian movement was studded with such brilliant names as Isaac Newton, John Locke, John Biddle, and, for a time, William Penn. But the man who deserves to be credited as the actual founder of the Unitarian Church in England was Theophilus Lindsey, a Church of England clergyman turned liberal.

Laying aside the traditional white surplice of his office, Lindsey conducted the first "official" Unitarian service in a London auction room. A large congregation, including

Benjamin Franklin and Joseph Priestley, participated in the drastically revised order of service. The date was April 17, 1774.

Lindsey's motivations can be best understood by reviewing the assertions which he described as the unifying bonds of the new Unitarian Church in England:

> "That there is One God, one single person, who is God, the sole creator and sovereign lord of all things;
> "That the holy Jesus was a man of the jewish nation, the servant of this God, highly honoured and distinguished by him; and,
> "That the Spirit, or Holy Spirit, was not a person, or intelligent being; but only the extraordinary power or gift of God, imparted, first (Acts i, 2) to our Lord Jesus Christ himself, in his life-time; and afterwards, to the apostles, and many of the first christians, to impower them to preach and propagate the gospel with success: and
> "That this was the doctrine concerning God, and Christ, and the holy Spirit, which was taught by the apostles, and preached to jews and heathens." *

This statement would strike most present-day Unitarians as mild, conservative, and tangential to current concerns. It must be appreciated, not for its present timeliness, but for the striking departures it represented in its own age. Moreover, it is the affirmation of a movement with direct and crucial ties to the emerging Unitarianism of America.

Coupled with Lindsey in the pioneering of liberal faith was the scientist, author, and clergyman, Joseph Priestley. Remembered best as the discoverer of oxygen, Priestley is judged by Wilbur to be "the most influential figure in the earlier history of the Unitarian movement in England." It is fair to extend the coverage of his influence to include

---

* Quoted by David B. Parke in *The Epic of Unitarianism*, Starr King Press, p. 47.

America. He gave intellectual brilliance and prodigious scholarship to the development of Unitarian religion, and, together with Lindsey, he stimulated a mushrooming growth of Unitarian institutions. With incredible energy, he spread his intelligence over the fields of preaching, pamphleteering, scientific research, and the espousal of many liberal and unpopular social and political causes, including the French Revolution. Inflamed by exasperated leaders of the established Church, a Birmingham mob chose Bastille Day, July 14, 1791, to attack and destroy Priestley's home, laboratory, library and Unitarian chapel. Priestley made a hairbreadth escape and found his way to London, where he immediately dispatched a sermon to be read to his congregation on the next Sunday using the text: "Father, forgive them; for they know not what they do."

Discouraged by the prevailing political and ecclesiastical climate, he made plans to quit England. In 1794 he sailed for the United States. There, in Northumberland, Pennsylvania, he gathered the first congregation in the new nation to call itself Unitarian.

The roots of American Unitarianism were already deep in the soil by the time of Priestley's arrival. Liberalizing breezes had long been blowing through the dour Calvinism of the colonies. Increasing numbers of ministers were calling for a greater use of reason in the interpretation of Scripture, for a questioning of the doctrine of original sin, for consideration of potential human goodness and the exercise of free will, and for belief in the unity of God against the orthodox doctrine of the Trinity. Priestley's presence on the scene expanded and hastened the progress of such liberalism, but it is to figures of the stature of Charles Chauncy, Jonathan Mayhew, and the pioneer Universalist, John Murray, that we should look for our origins in America. These men combined a bold humanism with their piety, a dauntless rationalism with their godliness. Determined at first to challenge only the dogmatisms of the dominant religious institutions, the liberal leaders found themselves pressed inexorably toward a genuine break. The chains of affiliation were finally shattered in the first quarter of the nineteenth century, and American Unitarianism emerged as a rapidly developing religious movement. As described by Parke *: "Thus freed from the shackles of tradition and circumstance, Unitarianism embraced Unitarian Christianity, Transcendentalism, and Naturalism in such rapid succession that the radicalism of Boston in 1819 was the conservatism of Cambridge in 1838 and anachronism of Chicago in 1880. Unitarianism also became the mind and pen of America as the Nation sought to discover where she was, where she had been, and where she was going. It was a magnificent century, one, like those of Jesus and Luther, to be re-lived and ploughed back into the future."

The Magnificent Century

The two colossi of religious liberalism in America were William Ellery Channing and Theodore Parker. Each could boast of sturdy Yankee lineage. The Parkers were citizens of Lexington for nearly two centuries before Theodore was born. The first Channing came to the colonies from Dorsetshire, England, in 1711. Each had one foot firmly planted in New England morality and the other in the Enlightenment's rationalism. Both were prodigious readers and scholars. Both were preachers of surpassing force.

Channing achieved his religious liberalism through an evolution from Calvinist training and belief. He believed in his youth that from the beginning God had elected those who would be saved and those who would be damned. His mature faith held that God bestows his love on all. He believed as a young man that human nature—including his own—was sunk in hopeless depravity. His espousal of Unitar-

* *The Epic of Unitarianism*, Starr King Press, p. 68.

ian religion was determined by his growing conviction that man's intrinsic moral sense gives him the power to perceive and choose the good.

Short of stature, slight of frame, supremely self-disciplined, Channing projected an image of humility, intellectuality, compassion, moral strength, and natural leadership.

In 1803 he turned down an invitation to become minister of the Brattle Street Church in Boston because it appeared to be too demanding a responsibility for his uncertain health. He took instead the far less prosperous Federal Street Church in Boston. His ministry there lasted until his death in 1842, compassing the entire period of emanating Unitarian organization in America. He preached with such effectiveness that the congregation quickly outgrew the building, making it necessary to construct a new and larger one, and his ministry became a continuous succession of great events. In his book-lined study were organized not only the American Unitarian Association, but new societies for the promotion of world peace, for adult education, for social service, for prison reform, for temperance. He was, says Van Wyck Brooks, "the father of half the reforms that characterized the Boston of his age." * Nothing was more compelling to Channing than the restoration of human dignity. He worked to rouse New England and the nation from the coma of Calvinism, with its crushing repudiation of man's faith in himself. He felt that religious leadership had become priestly rather than prophetic, while for many laymen the real god was commerce. He was determined to stir the imagination, light a fire of moral responsibility, and make the living of a life greater than the making of a living.

Using writing desk, pulpit, and lecture platform as tools, he worked his astonishing influence in three major areas: the liberalizing of theology, the implementing of social reform, and the stimulation of a literary and cultural renaissance.

* The Flowering of New England, E. P. Dutton & Co., p. 110.

It is now hard to believe that *any* sermon could create the stir roused by Channing's Baltimore address at the ordination of Jared Sparks in 1819. Yet, virtually every leading Unitarian minister made the dusty, exhausting journey to be there, and even before the sermon was delivered thousands of copies were prepared for circulation. Like Luther's Wittenberg theses, Channing's statements at Baltimore were destined to compel men to take a clear stand on fundamental religious problems. Unlike Luther's effort, it was widely known in advance that Mr. Channing would crystallize the issues.

According to orthodox theology, Channing said, man is left no freedom but the privilege of being damned. This is an insult both to God and man. "We object strongly," he went on, "to the contemptuous manner in which human reason is often spoken of by our adversaries.... We indeed grant, that the use of reason in religion is accompanied with danger. But we ask any honest man to look upon the history of the Church, and say, whether the renunciation of it is not still more dangerous."

Turning to his belief in the unity and benevolence of God, Channing said: "We cannot bow before a being, however great and powerful, who governs tyrannically. We respect nothing but excellence, whether on earth or in heaven. We venerate, not the loftiness of God's throne, but the equity and goodness in which it is established. We believe that God is infinitely good, kind, benevolent, in the proper sense of these words; good in disposition, as well as in act; good not to a few, but to all; good to every individual, as well as to the general system...."

Trying to summarize Channing's influence is like trying to summarize an epoch. Perhaps he did it best himself when he wrote: "I have lost no occasion for expressing my deep attachment to liberty in all its forms, civil, political, religious; to liberty of thought, speech, and the press, and of giving utterance to my abhorrence of all forms of oppression."

Fred G. Bratton says *: "A man of fervent yet dispassionate eloquence, impeccable character, and deep learning, Channing was the true representative of essential Unitarianism."

Channing was the fifth minister of the institution which, in its long and eventful history, has been known successively as The Church of the Presbyterian Strangers, the Federal Street Church, and the Arlington Street Church. As the thirteenth minister of this congregation, I extend an invitation to all readers of this book to vist our chapel, where you may see the graceful pulpit used by Channing for so many years to consecrate by the spoken word the dignity and power of the human spirit.

If Channing was the most influential figure yet produced by American Unitarianism, Theodore Parker was the most remarkable. At the apex of his preaching career in Boston's Music Hall, he spoke Sunday after Sunday to congregations of three thousand or more. His grandfather, Lexington's Captain John Parker, had delivered himself of one of America's immortal phrases, when in 1775 he said of the advancing British: "If they mean to have a war, let it begin here." Years later, when Theodore made up his mind to defy the Fugitive Slave Law, he recalled his grandfather's famous words and wrote: "I have had to arm myself. I have written my sermons with a pistol in my desk—loaded, a cap on the nipple, and ready for action. This I have done in Boston in the midst of the 19th century; been obliged to do it to defend the innocent members of my church, women as well as men. You know I do not like fighting . . . but what could I do? I was born in the little town where the first bloodshed of the Revolution began. My grandfather drew the first sword in the Revolution. With these memories in me, when a parishioner, a fugitive from slavery, a woman, pursued by kidnappers, came to my house, what could I do less than take her in and defend her to the last?"

* *The Legacy of the Liberal Spirit*, Scribner's, p. 200.

Parker made religion more than an exercise in church-manship. He took it from the pulpit onto the highways and into the cities and towns of burgeoning America. This is literally true in terms of his Herculean lecture tours, and figuratively true by reason of the subjects over which his mind ranged. He was a pathfinder in the practical applica-tions of religion, and a trail blazer in confronting secular issues with spiritual standards. He was, in the words of Henry Steele Commager, "the conscience of the North—of such men as Charles Sumner and John Hale and Abraham Lincoln, and of countless thousands of ordinary men and women who were troubled by the contrast between the faith they pro-fessed and the practices they tolerated." *

To Parker there were no exemptions from the validity of moral law; getting from Sunday to Monday, from the observances of religion to the practice of religion in every kind of human relationship, was the real business of the spiritual life. He recognized no gulf between the ecclesias-tical and the secular. To him they were one, and every hu-man being was bound by his religion to be deeply involved in the political, commercial, educational, and social improve-ment of the community.

His ministry began in West Roxbury, where he promised his congregation "to preach nothing as religion that I have not experienced inwardly and made my own." Many hours were spent in the well-stocked libraries for which Boston was noted. He nurtured his mind, ministered enthusiastically to the seventy families of his congregation, penned essays for Transcendentalist publications, and took an active interest in the affairs of the utopian Brook Farm community.

Then came Emerson's Divinity School Address: "Historic Christianity has fallen into the error that corrupts all at-tempts to communicate religion. As it appears to us, and as it has appeared for ages, it is not the doctrine of the soul,

* *Theodore Parker, Yankee Crusader,* Beacon Press, Preface.

but an exaggeration of the personal, the positive, the ritual.
It has dwelt, it dwells, with noxious exaggeration about the
person of Jesus. The soul knows no persons. It invites every
man to expand to the full circle of the universe, and will
have no preferences but those of spontaneous love. . . ."

Parker was stirred and depressed. Emerson's repudiation
of miracles, his man-centered sovereignty of spirit, his cele-
bration of "moral science," thrilled Parker. But Emerson had
turned his back on the Unitarian ministry and sought other
channels for his reforming energies. Parker brooded over
whether it would be necessary for him to do the same. He
decided to remain in the pulpit and to do everything in his
power to make the church an instrument for the very things
he and Emerson wanted.

By moving to Boston, he gained a national platform at the
Twenty Eighth Congregational Society. His sermons recognized the profound revolutions taking place in science and
philosophy. They were circulated, read, and discussed from
one end of the country to the other. Like Emerson, he
insisted that miracles proved nothing about religion. The
permanent truths of the spiritual life are confirmed by practice and experience. The forms of Christianity change; the
substance of religion remains. "If it could be proved," he
wrote, "that the gospels were a fabrication and that Jesus
of Nazareth never lived, Christianity would still stand firm
and fear no evil." Scientific truths do not rest on the word
of their discoverer. Gravity does not operate because Newton
said so. The same is true of the truths of religion. Confirm
them by experience, and not by whether Jesus spoke them,
or the Bible records them, or doctrine upholds them!

No part of my legacy as a Unitarian is more precious to
me than the portion created by Theodore Parker. He was
a prophet of righteousness, who believed, as I do, in the progressive development of the church. "The church," he said,
"should be the means of reforming the world. . . . It should

therefore bring up the ideas of the times, the sentiments of the times and the actions of the times, and judge them by the universal standard."

Parker petrified many of his fellow Unitarians, just as Emerson did, and strong efforts were made to expel him from the Unitarian ministry. It was a time for many of the more cautious Unitarians to attempt appeasement of the orthodox. Parker's outspokenness was an embarrassment—at the moment. It was a godsend to succeeding generations. Parker was the wave of the future for Unitarian religion in America. It is his spirit that has prevailed and thus preserved the only genius for which Unitarianism is fit—the genius which he himself described when he wrote: "Progressive development does not end with us; we have seen only the beginnings; the future triumphs must be vastly greater than all accomplished yet."

The Universalists

During the last half of the eighteenth century, a few isolated religious spokesmen in England and America began to preach the doctrine that it was unthinkable for God, as a loving Father, to damn any of his children everlastingly to hell, and only reasonable to suppose that God desires continuing growth and realization for all. How could a good God willfully plan the damnation of his offspring? The creedal assumption, formulated at Nicaea, must be in error. Even though the Council had pointed out that God's justice *required* the punishment of sin, it was self-evident that a good and perfect God created man to grow eternally in the goodness of his creator.

In the 1740's these "heretical" notions were preached in Pennsylvania by Dr. George de Benneville. In the 1760's similar ideas brought about the excommunication from Methodism of John Murray. These men were Universalists. They proclaimed the final harmony of the human soul with God.

Murray came from England to America, where in 1770 he presided over the founding of the Universalist Church of America. The birthplace of the movement was Good Luck, New Jersey. The founding fathers of Universalism avowed that "The love of God will ultimately prevail over the sinfulness of men." They were certain of this because they believed the love of God to be the most powerful force in the universe.

The Calvinist majority in the colonies was understandably disturbed by this obvious wandering from sound doctrine. It was to be expected from Unitarians, but this was a threat from a new quarter. There was immediate denunciation of the Universalists as an irresponsible lot bent on encouraging a life of reckless wickedness and ease, in the deluded belief that no matter what they did, they could count on escaping the tortures of hell. They are free thinkers and godless misinterpreters of a just God, said the Calvinist accusers; no better that Unitarians! In many New England villages, children were sternly instructed by their pastors and parents not to look a known Universalist in the eye if they wished to avoid having a curse brought upon them. Standing against the vehemence of the orthodox majority, Universalists stressed the ethical character of God. Their spokesmen maintained that God was by nature rational, loving, and redemptive. Sin, they said, was finite (reminiscent of Pelagius). Punishment was remedial, not vindictive. A future of social humanitarianism in later Universalist development was prepared by this early emphasis on the ethical and redemptive aspects of religion.

The movement grew very slowly, for the tempest of abuse was so strong that as late as 1800 only a handful of churches had been formed. Then there appeared on the New England scene a man of outstanding preaching ability. His name was Hosea Ballou, a courageous, scholarly, and extremely persuasive Universalist leader. He was born and reared a Baptist on a tiny New Hampshire farm. Somewhere along the line he was impressed with the "awful doctrine," as Universalism was called, and accepted the pulpit of Boston's School Street Universalist Church.

In 1803 he issued the celebrated *Winchester Profession,* which became the standard expression of Universalist views. In it he emphasized the Universal Fatherhood of God and the example and leadership of Jesus. It represented not only a further rupture with orthodoxy, but a distinct alteration of John Murray's tenets. Murray held orthodox beliefs about atonement and Jesus' role as divine atoner. By the time Ballou finished expanding his views in a book entitled *A Treatise on the Atonement,* he had effectively demolished atonement as a Universalist concept. He greatly expanded the loving God idea and the emphasis on the brotherhood of man. He added the phrase, "Salvation by Character." As for the punishment of sin, he stated that it was instant, constant and inevitable; *but* it was not everlasting, for the self-evident reason that everlasting punishment makes no sense. Unless punishment has *character* for its purpose, it is vicious and cruel. The only defensible reason for punishment is growth in righteousness. He asked, "Is God any less intelligent than a parent? Would a parent see any point in punishing a child forever? Would that improve the child?"

Thus Ballou made a statement which was as "Unitarian" as any of his time. His thought matched Channing's to a remarkable degree, with the added luster that it anticipated many of the things Channing would say in subsequent years. Most of the Universalist ministers followed Ballou's lead, making their movement an organized unitarian body some fifteen or twenty years before Unitarians, as such, gave themselves an official form.

Sadly, there was never any enthusiasm among emerging Unitarian leaders for close ties with the embattled Universalists. From 1815 to 1840, as Unitarians were seceding from Congregationalists and Congregationalists were repudiating

Unitarians, the Universalists, whose cause was virtually identical on the issues involved, looked longingly for encouragement, cooperation, understanding, and fellowship from Unitarians. Universalism did not possess the social and cultural status of Unitarianism, and reinforcement was desperately needed. It was not forthcoming. Unitarians, for whatever reason, were unable to muster any enthusiasm for the beleaguered religionists who were their closest theological cousins.

The situation pained Hosea Ballou, who wrote a poignant sermon addressed to Unitarians. He selected the pertinent text: "Nevertheless, I have somewhat against thee." He wrote eloquently of the affinity of the two groups. He rehearsed their common aspirations and frustrations, and called for an intellectual and spiritual unity. He chided Unitarians for currying favor with groups much less friendly to Unitarian ideas while virtually ignoring Universalism. Many of us who patiently pressed for the merger which now has taken place feel that Hosea Ballou would have been very happy about our efforts.

During the latter part of the nineteenth century, Universalism, like Unitarianism, was deeply stirred by the rise of critical Bible study. Bible-centered Universalism gave way gradually to philosophical Universalism. Max A. Kapp, a leading Universalist spokesman, wrote: "Darwinianism (from 1859 on) posed a challenge to all Bible-centered faith: Universalism quickly, but not without pangs, accepted the implications of the theory of evolution and other scientific findings. ... A marked shift of emphasis has gradually taken place so that 'salvation' no longer suggests to most Universalists an event in the after-life, but a process of self-fulfillment and social transformation."

As late as 1899 a Universalist statement of faith adopted in Boston reads: "We believe in the Bible as containing a revelation from God." But by 1935 a profession approved in

Washington states: "We avow our faith in the authority of truth, known or to be known." It is impossible to miss the broadening of view inherent in these statements.

Actually there was the same degree of theological variety among Universalists as among Unitarians. There were theists, humanists, naturalists, and mystics. There were Universalists who preferred an exclusive identification with Christianity, and Universalists who would divorce themselves from Christianity altogether. All Universalists came to accept what they called the "liberty" clause, which meant simply that no creedal test might be used for determining who should or should not be a Universalist.

I happen to be very fond of the Universalist name. The Unitarian name is precious to me because of the significance given to it by history. But simply as a word, laying aside for a moment the aura of history, it does not posses the magnificent, contemporary fitness of Universalism. It was a bit awesome to contemplate calling ourselves Unitarian Universalists or Universalist Unitarians (one wag has suggested taking the first two syllables of Universalist and the last three syllables of Unitarian, and combining them), but I personally worked to retain both names in the merged denomination; the one for its four-hundred-year saga of struggle for religious liberty and rationality, the other for the bold manner in which it points ahead, not to Christian man, Buddhist man, western man or eastern man, but to *universal* man.

When the merger took place, it united more than six hundred Unitarian local units with nearly four hundred Universalist congregations into a continental total of one thousand churches and fellowships. Since both denominations had what is called "congregational" polity, there was no disruption at the community level. Congregational polity means simply that the seat of authority is in the local church or fellowship, rather than in a synod, or bishop. It is the democratic principle in action in religion.

Both denominations had various regional and continental agencies and organizations. It is taking a good deal of patience, and possibly several years, to fit the pieces of this puzzle together. The two major administrative and service agencies, the American Unitarian Association and the Universalist Church of America, became a single headquarters at 25 Beacon Street in Boston.

I favored merger because I believe that its over-all result will be to strengthen the free church in its fundamental tasks. The liberal church should be one of the most modern and realistic of institutions. It should seek every legitimate means to rationalize and invigorate its internal administration. Combining the supplementary and complementary energies of Unitarians and Universalists is a logical move in this direction. The broader our base becomes, the more likely it is that we will do an effective job of imparting creative and moral inspiration to people's lives. The liberal church must be a society of free individuals. The greater the invasions of freedom and civil liberty in the larger community, the more necessary it becomes to cherish and enlarge the ideal freedom of the smaller religious community. Obviously, this cannot happen by accident. It requires intelligent planning and wise organization. In the modern world, freedom is threatened by adulteration, but it is also weakened by prosaic institutional arrangements. The Universalist-Unitarian merger is, in my opinion, an imaginative venture, in keeping with progressive, modern approaches to institutional life. It enlarges our horizons and invigorates the general climate of liberal religion.

The vital role of the liberal church is that of leavening. We must be the yeast of freedom which is forever working and increasing. We must be the bearers and breeders of freedom in the world. For us, denominational arrangements are not matters of authority, but effective implementations of the services we require and the causes we espouse. Authority does not inhere in councils or associations, but only in the consistency and adequacy of evidence in any proposal or proposition, and in demonstrations of character and competence on the part of individuals charged with leadership and responsibility. Thus titles and positions bestow no automatic power. Free men and women do not bow before offices. Respect is not accorded to positions as such. For the sake of the creative uses of freedom, we devise organizations, groups, agencies, offices, and positions. These are established, not to restrict, or limit, or circumscribe freedom, but to enable us to reach out beyond present customs and boundaries into unexplored areas, and to do so with maximum effectiveness. This requires maturity, not only in the individual, but in the techniques of administration and organization. The institution must grow along with the people who comprise it! I look upon a merger as a sign of maturity and a promise of growth.

The development of the actual merger is a most interesting success story. For more than a century the two groups grew increasingly conscious of one another, and their separate histories are notched with efforts to effect a closer relationship. A favorite joke among our late nineteenth-century forefathers alleged that Universalists believe God is too good to damn man, while Unitarians believe man is too good to be damned. On more than a dozen occasions resolutions were introduced calling for union of the two movements. Somehow, the practicalities of getting together dampened whatever ardor there was. In 1899 a motion adopted by both bodies established a joint committee to "seek coordination— not consolidation; unity, not union." There were no major results. In 1908 a National Federation of Religious Liberals was established. Its membership included Unitarians, Universalists, Quakers, and the Central Conference of American Rabbis. Little came of the effort. In 1923 Universalists were courted by the National Convention of Congregational Churches, and each group appointed a Committee on Comity

and Unity. Four years later, the Universalist Committee met
with an interested group of Unitarians to discuss setting up a
Congregational-Universalist-Unitarian organization; but the
whole move fell through because Universalist sentiment favored a Universalist-Unitarian structure. By 1933 still another council was incorporated in Massachusetts known as
the Free Church of America. Nearly one hundred Universalist and Unitarian congregations affiliated, along with one
Methodist church, one Independent church, and three Community churches. It was never possible to raise enough money
for either a staff or a program (the word "Free" was apparently interpreted in a financial as well as ideological sense),
so the movement withered.

In 1947 a joint Universalist-Unitarian commission was established to lay the groundwork for Federal Union, and after
an overwhelmingly favorable plebiscite among the churches,
the commission was instructed to present a practical plan.
By 1951, the commission was ready to recommend an immediate union in the fields of religious education, publications,
and public relations, with a gradual trend toward complete
merger. The report was ratified by both denominations. The
Council of Liberal Churches (Universalist-Unitarian) was organized in 1953. Meanwhile, the youth groups of the respec-
tive bodies voted to dissolve their separate structures and
merge immediately into a single movement. The result was
the Liberal Religious Youth organization, which has since
demonstrated with enthusiasm that mergers are easy for those
under twenty-five. Mergers are also apparently less trouble-
some to those concerned with religious education, and the
educational division of the Council of Liberal Churches func-
tioned with marked success. The recommendation was then
made and accepted that a commission be set up to bring the
question of *complete* merger to a head.

Merger has now been effected. The two separate denominational structures became one in May, 1960, in Boston.

FIVE

CHRISTIAN OR MORE THAN CHRISTIAN?

All creatures weak or strong,
Great or small,
Seen or unseen,
Near or far,—
May all be blessed with peace.
Let all-embracing thoughts
For all that lives be thine.

SUTTA-NIPATA

W E HAD driven through the night, crossing the Mohave
Desert by moonlight. At dawn we were about one
hundred miles from Los Angeles. I switched on the car radio
to hear the six o'clock news. The announcer's words sent
chills up my spine. The Nuri Said government in Iraq had
fallen with the suddenness and violence of a tornado. The
king, crown prince, and prime minister—all staunch friends
of the West—were dead. Mobs raged in the streets of Baghdad. It was summer, 1958.

To me, this was personal. Less than a year before I had
greeted another dawn in those same Baghdad streets. I had
sweated my way through the cars, pedestrians, horses, don-
keys, camels, pushcarts and bicycles. I had felt the swelter
of a blinding Iraqi sunrise. I could imagine all too vividly
the horror of the fanatical lynch-bent crowds.

Iraq is a Moslem country and the troubles besetting us

73

there, as in so many places, have origins in momentous human movements involving, among other factors, the religious beliefs and aspirations of people determined to have a different and better life.

What is a Unitarian Universalist's approach to the world's vast pattern of religions? Has liberal religion grown beyond Judeo-Christianity and become something more universal? Or, is it merely a branch of the Christian church which views without prejudice or missionary yearnings the spiritual traditions of others?

In Boston, on May 25, 1958, there occurred a memorable clarification of the Unitarian position as approved by a majority of the official delegates attending the annual meeting of the American Unitarian Association. The resolution stated that Unitarians "cherish the historic Judeo-Christian heritage of Unitarianism; affirm the universal sources and inspiration of modern Unitarian faith; and express the hope that all religious truth seekers may come together in the spirit of freedom, each contributing his highest insights to the common universal quest for truth."

If we are to be true to our genius for development, it could not be otherwise. The sudden, dramatic advent of the space age is but another urgent reminder of our world's need for a new approach to faith, one that feeds the great hungers of the human spirit without asking us to divide into hostile sects or split our minds into halves. The absence of such a faith—a faith expressed in the idiom of our age, at peace with its scientific methods and discoveries, awakening a real and deep interest in the soul, appealing to the highest and profoundest sentiments of our nature, permeating every facet of our being, and directing its enormous powers into channels that are creative and uniting—this lack is a great spiritual tragedy in our troubled world. I could not remain within the Unitarian Universalist fold unless I

felt that we were genuinely striving to build and demonstrate
such a faith. If I had to wrap a sectarian label around me, I
could not honestly accept it. I am willing to call myself a
Christian only if in the next breath I am permitted to say
that in varying degrees I am also a Jew, a Hindu, a Moslem,
a Buddhist, a Stoic, and an admirer of Akhenaten, Zoroaster,
Confucius, Lao-Tse and Socrates.

Channing was thinking only of Christianity when he said:
"We must shun the spirit of sectarianism as from hell. We
must shudder at the thought of shutting up God in any denomination." I, as a present-day Unitarian Universalist,
would extend the sentiment to include all the world's religions. Overwhelmingly, man's organized faiths—from Christianity to Communism—still remain bastions of the tense,
closed, heresy-hunting mind. I cannot choose for others, but
I can choose for myself. I can give my loyalty to a religious
institution whose aim is to unite the universal sources of
man's inspiration. For me such an institution *must* be more
than Christian.

There are dangers in this approach, and not those imag-
ined by one of my anonymous correspondents who continually tries to save my soul—by mail—because I do not accept
the exclusive saviourship of Christ. The dangers are inherent
in any reach that may exceed one's grasp. What I and most
of my co-religionists are today striving to achieve can easily
become a leaky bucket for sloppy thinking. It can be a way
of avoiding genuine issues in a fog of aimless and untested
benevolence. It is not difficult, at a distance, to build illusions about the other great religions. We are close enough to
Christianity to be realistic about its excesses, its egotisms, its
irrationalities, and its dogmatisms, but when we speak of the
far-away faiths—Islam, Buddhism, Hinduism—our voices tend
to take on a hushed tone. Our eyes acquire a starry glow.
Somehow we are not impressed that these, too, have their

shocking excesses, egotisms, irrationalities and dogmatisms. We are justifiably upset about Christian encroachments on the public schools and on the institutions of government, but these are relatively mild and timid compared to the invasions, say, of the *mullahs* into the civic privacy of peoples in Moslem lands.

It is very attractive for us to think of ourselves as a bridge for the world's many religions. After all, we have no special myths to defend, no creeds to enforce. We are open to all that is ethically best in the world's religions, and through freedom, reason, and tolerance we feel prepared to touch each of the great faiths and draw together their moral fervor. It is a grave mistake, however, to view this as a recreational task. Most of the hungry, diseased, and superstition-ridden folk—and they are the vast majority of the world's peoples— haven't the vaguest idea what we are talking about. I am only saying that it is extremely important for us to *know* what *we* are talking about.

We speak over and over again of our acceptance of change, and we are properly critical of those who resist change. Yet the kind of change we know and understand is comparatively mild, orderly and polite. There are vast areas of the world where change, when it comes, is like a volcano or an earthquake. It strikes with formidable fury and vengeance. Most of us have known very little of that kind of change.

When the General Assembly of the Unitarian Universalist Association met in Chicago in May, 1963 a schism arose regarding a proposed amendment recommending a militant support of the burgeoning civil rights feeling in the country, that fellowship be refused to churches which did not include in their statement of purpose any denial of membership on the basis of color. It seemed to me then, and more so at this writing, that opponents of the amendment, who were able to defend their position, based their arguments on the question of polity of the congregations as opposed to a strengthening of the powers of the association. To me a great opportunity was lost to stand forthrightly in the mainstream of the civil rights movement, and we were made to appear as fools haggling over semantics while the world went on without us, including, incidentally, the Presbyterian Church of America.

But in regard to the desire of Unitarian Universalists to play a universalizing role in the world community of faith, I am calling attention simply to the pitfalls of romanticizing the task. We must be careful how we tread in an area not yet very real to us, and it would be a sobering error to assume that we of the western Unitarian Universalist fellowship are *now* prepared to live in the world community. We are not. At the most rudimentary level, the unvarnished sights, sounds, smells, passions and credulities of the vast bulk of the world community would frighten and perhaps physically sicken us if we were thrown suddenly into their midst.

What we do have to our credit is an honest desire to play a useful, constructive, uniting role. We will learn soon enough that some of our present notions about spiritual unity and global religious fellowship are realizable only in part, over long periods of time, and as a result of infinite patience. Basically, ours is a nature "to seek peace and pursue it." We will develop a more agonized appreciation of how unreal peace can seem to hungry men who have been exploited from time out of mind. We will increasingly discover that world community is not an abstraction about which we can make inspiring poems, but a fearsome concreteness of honesty and corruption, cleanliness and dirt, kindness and barbarism, hope and hunger. This consciousness will grow in us, and we are right in anticipating it, because the world community is a reality and we must begin to treat it as such. We will become better, stronger people than we are—sadder and wiser. We will make more room in our hearts and minds for tragedy because limited tragedy is

one of the hallmarks of the present world community, and
total tragedy could become its end result.

We will not desert our humanism. Instead, it will become
a sturdier, more reliable humanism because it learns to accept the very real presence of despair in people's lives. We
will not forsake our optimism, but it will become an optimism based more on man' ability to surpass his errors and
cruelties than on the possibility of completely abolishing
them.

The arc of America's success and power is still ascending,
and we religious liberals, along with our fellow Americans,
have much to learn about the use of ideas to nourish the
human spirit. The United States, by all exterior standards,
is a supercolossal power and Americans still expect the rest
of the world to be properly impressed. In this country in general, we assume that there must be a moral flaw in those who
do not instantly recognize the rightness and piety of our
intentions. We are beginning to sense, perhaps, a flaw in our
infallibility as now and then we experience setbacks in the
world.

To our everlasting credit, Unitarian Universalists have
been sufficiently sensitive to identify the weaknesses in our
national religiosity. We have not been alone in this; but we,
and others, have spoken candidly of the shameful tendency to
conscript God as a tribal deity to safeguard and protect the
interests of particular nations, especially our own; a God
who is "on our side," a God who can be summoned to dis-
comfit "atheistic communism." We have been keen enough
to sense that a religion which is merely an accessory of national purpose is a religion that even the Soviets could tolerate. We have been trying to point out to our more bemused
fellow citizens that glib talk about our Christian spirit and
godliness is dangerous because it obscures the real creative
need. Yet, we have thus far contributed only haltingly to the
actual labor of creation.

There is no mystery about the need in our world community. It is for an understanding of man himself, as an individual within his collective civilization. And it must be an understanding lacking illusions enough to measure our limitations within a universe incomprehensibly greater than ourselves, and to estimate our potentials for fashioning a sane, productive life within that frame. It must also be an understanding frank enough to accept man as part of a naturalistic order, a creature who first emerged from the animal world as a caprice of nature—subject to destructive impulses that can be elaborated by the intricate cunning of his brain; but also a creature with transforming capacities of thought, imagination, self-awareness and heroism. Further, it must be an understanding courageous enough to assert that man is part of a moral order outside of which he loses his meaning, but within which there must be a steady demolition of the divisive walls of competitive theology.

We were suitably alarmed a few years ago when the World Council of Churches met in Evanston to proclaim impertinently that Christ is "the hope of the world." Our sense of the fitness of things was disturbed. We know that a theological Christ is not the hope of a world made up in large part of people who will never be Christians. We know that the world's hope rests not in Christ or Moses or Buddha or Krishna or Mohammed or Lenin, but in the ability of their devotees to live side by side on a shrinking planet. Strangely enough, an old adversary has suddenly become an eloquent ally. We find Arnold Toynbee speaking our lines: "In the world in which we now find ourselves, the adherents of the different living religions ought to be readier to tolerate, respect, and revere one another's religious heritages because, in our generation, there is not anyone alive who is effectively in a position to judge between his own religion and his neighbor's. . . . If we do not feel that we can wait for Time to do its discriminating work, we are confessing to a lack of faith in the truth and value of the religion that happens to be ours. On the other hand, if we do have faith in it, we shall have no fear that it will fail to play its full part in helping human souls to enter into communion with the presence behind the phenomena and to bring themselves into harmony with this Absolute Reality. The missions of the higher religions are not competitive; they are complementary. We can believe in our own religion without having to feel that it is the sole means of salvation." *

Those of us who dream of an onrushing day when all mankind will become even as we—American-style Unitarian Universalists—need to take this new Toynbee to heart. He is talking to us as well as to others.

For ourselves, we must have a view of life that sustains us and prepares us for living in the thorny world community of which we are a part. But we must not assume that we can immediately communicate our religious point of view to our world neighbors in convincing particulars. After all, we are not overly successful in communicating it to much closer neighbors here at home. We must, in fact, strip ourselves of the irrelevant belief that, for their own good, all men should accept our definition of what is rational. We must divest ourselves of the basically smug assumption that human progress and happiness are possible only in terms of "our realities."

There is in this strange new world community a temptation to spiritual imperialism, and it entices us as well as others. We criticize our crusading Christian friends partly out of annoyance that they are making more difficult an ultimate conquest by our own superior product.

Liberal religion is something that can and does help us to become useful citizens of the emergent world community, but it is not a mystique for the world as a whole any more than Billy Graham's fundamentalism. Unitarian Universal-

* *An Historian's Approach to Religion,* Oxford University Press, pp. 297-298.

ism is a source of inspiration through which we can divest ourselves of sectarianism in a comprehensive as well as denominational sense, and through which we can make genuine, even if modest, contributions of love, justice and intelligence to the larger whole. But this source is meaningful to us because we are the kind of people we are, and not because it is the only true insight available to enlightened human minds.

For me, one of the most evocative aspects of our religion is its ability to be always in transition, always "coming out" of where it has been in favor of new and exciting spiritual adventures. Dean Inge once remarked that traditional Christianity "is geocentric . . . earth-centered." We are becoming more and more aware that we live not in a geocentric but a galactic universe, and that the appeal of traditional Judeo-Christian theology grows progressively weaker.

Channing's celebrated sermon at Baltimore was an assertion of Unitarian Christianity. He denied the doctrines of the Trinity, predestination, and depravity, but otherwise remained, in a parochial sense, a Christian. In the intervening decades our religious teaching has steadily broadened in its conscious appreciation of our debt to the rationalism and stoicism of the Greek and Roman philosophers, to the Renaissance, to the French and English Enlightenment, and, above all, to the heritage of modern science. As Dr. George Stoddard said a few years ago: "Science has won all the arguments with the theologians, and will continue to do so. This sounds quite flat-footed but in the perspective of one hundred years it will probably be verified."

The Judeo-Christian tradition will continue to play a vital role in our religious education, but it can never again be the essence, as it once was, of the training given our children and adults.

At our meetings in May, 1957, Yale's professor of Natural Philosophy, Dr. Henry Margenau, summarized the prevalent outlook in Unitarian churches and fellowships when he described man's fate as hanging precariously upon our ability to conquer a cultural lag that is laden with archaic religious conceptions. He spoke of how great scientific advances inevitably blow the winds of change in two directions: technological and cultural. We have achieved an easy familiarity with the first. Space travel seems no more unlikely to us than stereophonic phonographs. The second aspect is far less a part of the normal play of our minds. Incisive scientific discoveries involve new theories of reality. Often they undermine views previously held to be "just plain common sense." Frequently they call for revisions of our beliefs about the universe and our theories of knowledge and nature. All aspects of human relationship are eventually affected by such discoveries, including religion. But the movement is slow and tortured. Technology rushes ahead. Culture lags. Religion loiters. The unique talent of Unitarian Universalism is acceptance of the scientific *method,* which involves not merely a willingness to cope with technological results, but an eagerness to explore the results in terms of faith, worship and morality. "The accent of science," said Dr. Margenau, "shifts from discovery to creation. It adds organization to facts. Science can and must deal with values." Liberal religion realizes that science does not deal simply with facts; it propels the human enterprise by hopes and dreams that transcend facts.

The famed astronomer, Dr. Harlow Shapley of Harvard, raises with remarkable clarity and literary skill the issue of man's spiritual response to the expanding, cosmic findings of science. He recalls how the prophets of ancient Israel gloried at times in the magnificence of the universe, which in their time was centered on man. Scientifically, however, those days were very early. "What the inquiring mind has since uncovered," he writes, "would have been incredible if revealed to the ancient prophets. Their vision was, we now see, myopic. Our vision is doubtless also deficient, but at least we recognize that we are taking part in a play far grander than foretold in ancient time. The advance notices of two or three millennia ago greatly underestimated the cosmic drama. Reverence then had to be supported with imaginings and superstition. But the accepted facts of now far transcend the fictions of not so long ago. So it seems, at any rate, to those who look downward into atoms and the biological cell and upward to the stars. To be reverent, we now have no need of supernatural aid." *

If this appears to be boastful talk, Shapley offers the pride-shrinking thought that the inadequacies of the ancient religionists will probably be matched a century hence by the evidence that our present "advanced" concepts of the universe are primitive. "We hope for greater knowledge and sounder ideas in the future," says Shapley. "Deeper thoughts will surely come, wider spread of the senses, fuller appreciation of the functioning of the human brain, higher ambitions for men participating in the greatest operation of nature—an operation of cosmic dimensions that might simply be called Growth." †

Shapley is keenly aware that the modern cosmic outlook is strong and bitter medicine to many, who see in it only a dismal downgrading of man. But he speaks for most present-day liberal religions when he refers to the glory and *wonder* of the magnificent universe now unfolding. Man is an infinitesimally small and brief part of the mighty drama; the rules of the stars are hard; and the flow of time is irrevocable. But the lights exceed the shadows. "As rational practitioners of life and tentative interpreters of the cosmos, we deplore superstition—the last stronghold of the irrational. But thanks to man's reasoning, never before has hampering superstition been in retreat on so wide a front. Belief in the supernatural

* *Of Stars and Men,* Beacon Press, pp. 24-25.
† *Ibid.,* p. 25.

is tempered with thought. Rationalism has captured many
outposts in our necessarily continuous conflict with Tyranny
of the Unknown. We no longer need appeal to anything beyond nature when we are confronted by such problems as the
origin of life, or the binding forces of nucleons, or the or-
bits in a star cluster, or the electrochemical dynamics of a
thought, or some super-entity of the material universe. We
can assail all such questions rationally." *

The religion that commands my loyalty and enthusiasm
is concerned with returning to man's hands the holy fire that
was allowed to escape to heaven. This means a fervent espousal of reason that transcends all parochialisms, even as
impressive a one as the Judeo-Christian tradition. Either we
are "more than Christian" or we are just another portion of
religion's lag.

The liberal spirit in religion has emerged from the orthodoxies of many different faiths. It insists that the highest
method of religion is freedom; that its maturest guide is
reason; that its ultimate test is character; that its broadest
spirit is fellowship; and that its all-encompassing goal is
service. This spirit has appeared in greater or lesser degree in
all the great faiths. It emerged in Hinduism as early Buddhism, then later as the Brahmo-Samaj. It appeared in cultic
Judaism as the ethical emphasis of the early prophets and
then again in the efforts of Jesus to simplify and purify
Judaism's moral imperatives. It sprang to life in ancient
Greece under the glowing guidance of a Socrates. Its story is
that of bursting out of the cocoons of the religions men build
for themselves. All the great faiths as we see them in the
world today are a mixture of the two contradictory impulses; the thrust to the sectarian, the narrow, the particular,
and the thrust to the universal, the all-embracing, the comprehensive.

Invariably, the narrow instinct of each religion is chained

* *Ibid.,* p. 157.

to its now-myopic past, to the hard crust of its "exclusive" revelations. The devotees of God's incarnation in Christ *must* contend with the devotees of God's whisperings in the ear of Mohammed. But every faith also has its universalistic proclivity; one that is basically spiritual rather than mythical, ethical rather than doctrinal, social rather than sectarian. It is in this realm that all the great faiths are in fundamental harmony with one another:

> In Hinduism: "Systems of faith differ, but God is one."
> In Buddhism: "The good man's purpose is to increase the mercy, charity, kindness, and piety of all mankind."
> In Islam: "Fair is the dwelling of those who think not only of themselves but act with regard to the welfare of all."
> In Judaism: "Who gains wisdom: He who is willing to receive instruction from all sources."
> In Zoroastrianism: "Diversity of worship has divided the human race into many creeds. From among all their dogmas I have selected one—divine love."
> In Shintoism: "Regard heaven as your father, earth as your mother, and all things as your brothers and sisters."
> In Confucianism: "Love cannot be outnumbered."
> In Christianity: "Let us therefore follow after the things that make for peace and the things wherewith we may edify one another."

There is a distinctive note in each of the great religions. They cannot be better described than as the many strings of a harp. Their harmony flows from dealing with the same materials: human nature and human relationship. Their highest aspirations are universally human.

Unitarianism arose as the universalizing impulse within Judeo-Christianity, and grew in its awareness of kinship to the same impulse in all other great faiths. This is what led Emerson to the study of Asian religions and to their lasting imprint on his life and thought. This is what drew from his lips the unforgettable passage in the noted Divinity School Address on July 15, 1838: "Attach thyself not to the Christian symbol, but to the moral sentiment which carries innumerable Christianities, humanities and divinities in its bosom."

Channing, for all his devotion to a Christian identification, was moved to write: "Virtue is no local thing. It is not honorable because born in this community or that, but for its own, independent, lasting beauty. This is the bond of the universal church. No man can be excommunicated from it but by himself, by the death of goodness in his own breast."

Under the chairmanship of Dr. Frederick May Eliot, Unitarians established a Commission of Appraisal in 1934. Two years later the group produced its challenging report, saying: "What is needed is an association of free churches that will stand and fight for the central philosophy and values of liberal religion. . . . These churches . . . will be thoroughly emancipated from the sectarian spirit, from the tendency to set themselves up as small, select, superior groups of men and women to whom by some mysterious dispensation an exclusive gift of truth has been granted. They will cultivate an intensive sense of fellowship within their own ranks, but they will be keenly aware of the world-wide aspects of their liberal faith, recognizing the kinship of liberals across all barriers of race, nationality or traditional religious background. . . . They will not desire to 'Christianize the world,' because they believe that religion is deeper and more significant than any of its historical forms—even the Christian."

No document has ever been more prophetic. It recognized and gave added force to an unmistakable trend. It reads today like a spiritual blueprint of the kind of world most Unitarian Universalists want keenly to help create.

As my colleague, Dr. Donald Harrington of New York's Community Church, has recently expressed: "Truth is not

Christian or Jewish, Hindu or Buddhist. What is true for one man is true for all men. Just as there is no such thing as Christian medicine, or Jewish biology or Hindu psychology or Buddhist sociology, so there is no such thing as sectarian truth. Truth is universal. It is progressively discovered and formulated by men of all faiths and philosophies, and, when it is substantiated, it is the same for all men everywhere."

Mid-century Unitarian Universalism is girded with a message of religion's universal truths and a method based on universal needs. It affirms the oneness of the universe, the oneness of the human family, the oneness of discovered and discoverable truth, the universal validity of free inquiry, and the dawn of universal man. We are not anti-Christian any more than we are anti-Moslem, or anti-Jewish. In fact, we are not anti-anything except ignorance, superstition, dogmatism, bigotry, poverty, injustice, tyranny and disease.

It is our hope that the dimensions of our liberal faith may stretch to meet the spiritual requirements of the age now emerging. It remains for us to transform our faith into an adequate working force whose energies will not rest or cease to mature as long as brotherhood, righteousness and peace are the poorly realized dreams rather than the realities of our common life.

The words of the late, great A. Powell Davies are symbolic of the religion that fills my imagination with wonder: "The world is now too dangerous for anything but truth, too small for anything but brotherhood. A character is no longer really good that stops short of the universal claim upon it."

SIX

WHERE IS GOD?

...the question is not whether man returns to religion and believes in God but whether he lives love and thinks truth.

ERICH FROMM, *Psychoanalysis and Religion*

ONE of the most perplexing aspects of liberal religion to the outsider is God. It is simply beyond the ken of many to comprehend a church in which there is lacking a united, doctrinal conception of God. Students of religion are familiar with gods of many forms and kinds, but most laymen are not students of religion. They are believers or nonbelievers, and for them the word God is all of a piece or it is nothing.

In reality, the gods of men are of indefinite number and variety. What God may or may not be, I will discuss presently. For now let us deal with the insights that come to anthropologists and psychologists when they acquaint themselves with a number of cultures in varying stages of development. Gods are not fixed, objective realities, and only a few have constancy and continuous significance. Most change in astonishing and confusing ways. All bear vitally on human interests and habits.

At the most primitive levels of life, uncommon objects such as strangely shaped boulders, gnarled trees, albinos, maniacs, giants, pygmies, and the like, are generally considered to be under the spell of special spirits, or gods, or as being themselves spirits of unique power. A similar significance is attached to wind, waterfalls, eclipses, volcanoes, and earthquakes. Primitive man draws no clear distinction between what we call the real and the dream worlds, or between sense perceptions and the workings of imagination. He knows nothing of an ordered and law-abiding system of Nature. Anything may transform itself and become something else. Marvels occur throughout life. Men may become animals, and animals men. A cave may come alive and speak. The spirits animating this endless riot of weirdness are infinitely varied and numberless, and they are generated out of transient experience. They may live for a moment, a day, or an age, according to the particular substance they embody.

The gods, or spirits, are offspring of things that happen and minds that react. Because some events are experienced regularly and with crucial significance, their spirits are more urgently familiar, important and lasting. Obvious examples are the sun, rain, the birth of human and animal young, and the growth of food. But the world in which these experiences occur is so uncertain and fraught with danger that even the most familiar events are filled with tension and foreboding wariness. Every crisis of birth or harvest is a moment of emotional stress. Whatever grips the attention of preliterate people, especially a situation which regularly recurs, is likely to take on the character of spirit.

As to whether the primitive mind distinguishes between the object and its inhabiting spirit is a problem on which scientists have achieved no general agreement; just as agreement is lacking in our scientific culture as to whether the mind is different from the body or is merely the body functioning in a special way. The prevailing psychological view is that we are "organisms-displaying-mental-ability." This is not, however, universally accepted. It should not be puzzling, in view of scientific disagreements about the nature and role of mental activity, that prescientific peoples are unable to make clear, harmonious statements about the nature of spirits and their relation to objects.

In general, only the stronger, more impressive, more permanent spirits deserve to be called gods. They alter with the shifting fortunes of their followers, and they reflect the changing fates and cultures of their people. The Spirit of the Tribe becomes God. There are many gods concerned with the different enterprises and functions of the tribe, but in time there is also a superior divinity—such as Zeus for example—who presides over all.

The two most important changes in man's theological odyssey are the humanizing and universalizing of the grand God. It is in Greece and Israel that we see this process most clearly and impressively. In each case the earlier divinities were animals, or spirits in the animals. Most conspicuous were the bull and the sheep. Somehow the life of the group was felt to depend especially upon them. Sacrifice, the ancestor of worship, consisted of slaughtering and eating the sacred animal for the purpose of renewing the vitality and cohesiveness of the group. As the well-being of the tribes fell more and more into the hands of self-conscious human leaders—whether as judges, warriors or kings—the increased awe felt for dominant men, and a growing dependence on them, created a pattern for the emergence of manlike deities. The animal gods did not suddenly disappear. They were still active participants in temple rites long after Yahweh and Zeus were commonly conceived in kingly form. It took generations of persistent prophets to cleanse the popular religion of its primitive throwbacks, and to elevate it to the level of high deities whose characters were as lofty as those of the best of men.

This prophetic struggle began with denunciation of totems and other nature gods, and grew, through the efforts of such figures as Amos, Hosea and Isaiah, to the solemnization of

justice, mercy and wisdom as the traits of God. Centur
bitter conflict were involved in establishing a pattern oi
exalted human behavior as being characteristic of the Divine. The humanizing of God emerged with the growing
realization that moral qualities were of great importance in
the rulers of a nation. Only with the achievement of this
insight could God be conceived as judge and king, exercising
moral sway over the affairs of his people.

It was a task of even more tortuous difficulty to bring about
the universalization of the gods. The Hebrew Yahweh clung
stubbornly to his local, provincial nature until the Exile.
The refugees from Jerusalem insisted upon carrying some of
their native soil with them so that they might stand upon it
to gain recognition from their god. Only when it became a
physical impossibility to do this—because of numbers—did
the belief arise that Yahweh was powerful even outside his
native domain. The conviction that Yahweh was the God
of lands other than Palestine, that, in fact, he was Lord of
the entire earth, developed on the strength of Hebrew experiences with foreign exile, travel, commerce, and diplo-
matic relations with neighboring peoples. From the prophets
of Israel came the magnificently original idea that Yahweh
was indeed the God who ruled over Egypt, Syria and Baby-
lon, as well as Zion. The prophets were geniuses because
they understood the necessity of universalizing their God to
the full scope of the world in which his people lived and
strived. Otherwise, Yahweh would be diminished and de-
graded to the dimensions of the tiny, vanquished land of
Palestine. The boldness of such a claim is history's clearest
expression of the immensely vital and unique spiritual genius of the Hebrews.

To be sure, the idea of Yahweh's relation to other peoples
remained superficial for a long time. The Hebrews conceived
of his influence on their neighbors as being implemented by
stratagems, by shrewdly sown confusions in the minds of

foreign rulers, and by subtle introductions of his will into their secret thoughts. Others were not yet Yahweh's own, as were the Hebrews. His responsibility for Israel was still singular. The significance for religion's development was that the enlargement of Yahweh's sovereignty, whatever the limitations, was a novel achievement. The prophets raised God to a new level of moral influence. His power was no longer to be measured by the strength or affluence of his chosen followers, but by the rightness and righteousness of men's lives. This conviction came to full flower in Isaiah's teaching that Israel's cause depended more on her faith in God than on her military prowess.

With the elevation of reason as the supreme attribute of life, the Greeks climaxed their humanization of God. That which glorifies and dignifies man is wisdom. The source of order and justice in the state is wisdom. The individual's understanding of the world, and his ability to achieve moral competence, stem from wisdom. Reason and knowledge become practical through wisdom. Plato taught that a philosopher would make the best king, and that God is the perfect philosopher, the perfectly rational being. The Stoics made a complete and vital religion of the humanization and rationalization of God. Reason, the supreme principle, dwelt in all men. It observed no boundaries of race or nation. As the key to the right conduct of life, it was mankind's bond of kinship and brotherhood. Thus the Stoics were the first truly "international men." They were citizens of Greece by accident of birth, but they were citizens of the world by the nature of their being. Their God was not geographical but universal.

Stoicism was the harvest of Greek experience. Through travel, colonization, science and philosophy, the Greeks cultivated a cosmopolitan outlook. In her glorious era, Athens was the center for men of many races and cultures who were eager to mingle their quests for truths about humanity and

God. The flourishing of scientific and reflective thought prepared the way for the idea of a universal God. The Stoics crowned the effort by carrying the conception throughout the Mediterranean world as the zestful missionaries of a reasoned, spirited religious faith.

With Descartes the modern world began an examination of the idea of God matching in quality the independent metaphysics of the Stoics. Can the reality of God be established by abstract logical process of thought? Can the existence of God be proved by philosophy? The result has been most memorably summed up by Kant: human knowledge is incapable of supplying final verification for God's existence. Kant's method and the persuasiveness of his findings are so dependent upon the procedures introduced by Descartes (and followed by his successors for more than three centuries) that it is imperative to review Descartes' management of the problem.

The first order of business for Descartes was to institute the scientific method in philosophy. He began by making a heroic effort to cleanse his mind of all inherited ideas and acquired assumptions. Nothing was to remain but established and irrefutable facts. He arrived at what he felt was the one unquestionable fact of experience: his own consciousness of self. But this self was assumed to be the traditional soul, lodged in the forefront of the brain. With that assumption, the realm of experience was necessarily split in two. One part was the self or soul, with its thinking; the other part was the entire world of objects, other persons, and God. Through the centuries men have struggled to bridge the gulf between the self and other things. With things existing separately and outside, and with ideas existing as the thought processes of the self, there is no way to span the chasm between them and ensure that the impressions in the brain are true representations of objects outside the self. The soul, in brief, cannot be certain that its ideas of God are accurate confirmations of God's existence or nature.

The various schools of philosophers take up their positions on one or the other of the chasm's sides: those who rally to the self are the idealists, and they lean out over the brink to reach the reality they declare to be beyond their grasp; on the opposite side are the materialists who insist that the self should be disregarded, being at best a phantom description of one aspect of the physical world. Floating precariously in mid-air between the two are the so-called dualists, who assume the reality of both soul and external world and never succeed in explaining satisfactorily how the two get together.

God need not be a problem to the materialist since the question of a divine being is no more compelling than the question of a soul. Both can be explained as metaphorical descriptions of physical experience. Kant summarized the frustration of all idealists when he insisted that reason's quest for proof of God is doomed to failure. Yet, said Kant, it is a quest which reason can never desert. He dissected all the great historical arguments—the cosmological, the teleological, and the ontological—with the unrelenting will of one who is determined to know. In the end he concluded that though these arguments will continue to be used, they will always crumble when thoroughly probed. Reason compels the quest but can never resolve the dispute. There will continue to be as strong a case against God's existence as for it. Kant's judgment on centuries of philosophical toil was to declare a draw. The only possible means of confirming God's reality was to seek verification through other than scientific rules of evidence or philosophical rules of logic. All such efforts to find and experience God, in spite of reason's equivocation, came properly under the heading of mysticism. Access to God is thus claimed through feeling and superrational means. Mysticism is the legitimate outcome of the acknowledged failure of classical metaphysics. Men and women assert a genuinely satisfying and convincing experience of God, without the means of subjecting this experience to measurements of evidence or logic. They cannot explain the experience, but they have it; since the experience is more important to them than the explanation, they choose the former and bypass the latter.

People who think seriously and reflectively about their religious convictions are deeply affected by the intensity of this issue. Is it right to turn aside from the full implications of the scientific method when we reach the problem of God? Is mysticism a worthy answer to the seeming inability of empiricism to cope with the ultimate mystery of God? Nowhere is the genius of the liberal church better exemplified than in the manner in which this issue is treated.

God Is a Problem

Even to suggest, within the framework of an organized church, that God might be a problem is a scandal to many, bordering on blasphemy. Not so among us. God is a problem for several reasons; first, because God is a "word" used to cover a vast multiplicity of meanings. Normally, the word is used as if everyone understood the same things by it; but can anyone, with reasonable consideration, claim that Albert Einstein's God is the same as Oral Roberts'? This is one of the problems of God: a problem of definition, a problem of language, a problem of semantics. There is genuine pertinence in the remark of my colleague, Wallace Robbins: "Don't slap God on the back; you'll miss."

Another reason why God is a problem emerges from what people know or do not know about the historical evolution of God concepts. The God of a Hindu priest is a quite different product of spiritual development than the God of a Roman Catholic priest. Through the ages man's various divinities have been a splendid company, and it is a great pity that they are not better known. A deeper appreciation of their

richly diverse functions and natures would temper many of
the competitive hostilities between peoples of different beliefs. The gods of mankind can only be known by those who
take the trouble to investigate origins and comparative histories, and since so few have taken this trouble, God *is* a
problem in divisive misunderstanding and bitterness.

Still another problem is the symbolism of God. Religion
deals with great, sweeping issues of destiny. When you ask
someone how to get to the bus stop, you anticipate a simple,
direct answer. But when you ask "Where are we all going?"
you do not expect someone to answer "Omaha" as the man
in one of Sandburg's poems does. Religion strives for an
over-all account of the sum of things. It has an interest in
totality, and God is the symbol most commonly used to express this cosmic perspective. But, it is a tremendously large
and all-encompassing symbol. Within its misty infinities, it
is easy to become confused. Confused people lose their patience with one another. They find themselves contending
for concrete definitions, and in the name of such definitions,
massive slaughters have taken place.

Reasonable, temperate people come along who say that
such strife is senseless. There is no way to prove anything
about God, so why squander precious energies? It is better to
put the problem aside until we have more to go on. Meanwhile, we can turn our attention to matters which yield to
our current skills and knowledge. For the present, at least,
the proper study of man is man. Let religion throw its entire
and undistracted strength into the struggle to extricate man
from his present failings and dilemmas. Someday we may
know enough to make responsible statements about God. At
present it is not possible.

I have described here the view of a growing company of
sincerely religious persons both within and outside the Unitarian Universalist body. Yet, many are not willing to sus-
pend their speculations about God. The asking of ultimate

questions may be impractical, but one of reason's compulsions is the urge to ask.

We recognize from the start that it is undesirable to press for conformity of profession about the nature of God. As I have suggested, for some it seems better to leave the symbol "God" in abeyance until there is more to go on. For others, it is a symbol representing, however intangibly, the precious quest for deeper and deeper meanings. None of us tries to tell another what he should or should not believe about God, but every Unitarian Universalist assumes an obligation to know as fully as possible the facets of human experience out of which theologies arise.

Man has told himself many stories about human origins, destinies, and relationships to the forces he has called the gods and God. These stories have two common elements: they reflect the ordinary fears and strivings of daily life, and they recognize the existence of forces man may never actually touch or see but which must be taken into account in describing the reality of life. Inevitably, these stories raise puzzling questions. Is man but a meaningless speck in infinite wastes of time and space, a helpless victim of random forces, a careless product of sightless energies, a creature like Ernest Hemingway's "Old Man of the Sea," who catches the largest fish of his career only to have it devoured by sharks before he can bring it to shore? Are good and evil as casual, as coincidental, as impersonal as the catch and the shark? Is man, as Lewis Mumford has phrased it, "a smoking candle with a charred wick, giving no light beyond the pale of his own little niche: a poor flame flickering in a wind that will speedily extinguish it"?

Or is man the real center of divine attention, the wayward child of a loving deity, a creature who has flaunted his rebellious will in the face of a Father-God and placed his soul in eternal jeopardy? Has he, by his disobedience, thrust himself out of a Garden of Eden where he was at one with all creation? Is his nature both earthly and divine, but so steeped in the sins of assertiveness and pride that it cannot overcome damnation except through a gift of divine grace? Is it true that man can find the answers he seeks only if he prepares himself for another world and turns all his hopes and energies toward it? Does he begin his true life with death: the passage to an eternity of bliss or torment?

This is the story orthodox Christianity tells to the world, and with certain variations (some of them important) it is the story told by many religions. The notion that the world is a cave of darkness in which man is a prisoner forced to spend his days with his back to the light—this notion is far older than Christianity.

How does a man think his way through such dilemmas as the traditional myths pose? He thinks, quite naturally, within his own limits. Since his life appears to have a beginning and an end, he thinks of the universe in the same way. It, too, must begin and then cease. Man understands best the things which he himself has created. In an effort to understand the universe, he assumes that there must have been a creator who stands outside his creation and controls it. Man's earliest metaphysical thinking was done at a time when kings and despots ruled as tyrants with absolute authority over property, behavior, ideas, and even life. Representative democracy and the consent of the governed were nowhere in sight. Consequently, man tended to think of his gods or God as almighty, unchallengeable figures, like his kings.

It is difficult for most Unitarian Universalists to understand why people have continued through the ages to fashion God in the image of a despot. Even more to the point is the question of God as creator. If God is creator, was he himself uncreated? John Stuart Mill, in his celebrated autobiography, writes: "My father taught me that the question 'Who made me?' cannot be answered, since it immediately suggests the further question 'Who made God?' Here in this very simple sentence is the enormous fallacy in all the so-called proofs of God's existence as a First Cause. If everything must have a cause, then God too must be caused. If there is anything without a cause, it might just as well be you as God."

It was Bertrand Russell who, in a later commentary on Mill's conundrum, pointed out that it is like the Hindu's view of the world resting upon an elephant and the elephant resting upon a tortoise. When someone asks, "How about the tortoise?" the Indian says, "Let's change the subject."

The argument for God as creator, as Kant and many others have pointed out, is plainly unconvincing. Logic throws up no obstacle to the notion that the world came into existence without a cause. It is equally logical to consider that the universe has always existed, but the human imagination shrinks at these possibilities. The tendency to think in terms of beginnings and conclusions is strong; so man speculates about God as creator and first cause, and leads himself to the conviction that God, though in the midst of his creation, is separated from it by incalculable distance. God is part of man, yet dwarfs all men by his awful perfection. Is it not fair to say that such a God, in terms of reason, is actually more of a problem than the problems his existence is presumed to solve?

Baffled by the very mysteries he creates for himself, man, the ineffable theologian, plunges into further contradictions. On the one hand, God is pictured as pure spirit, nameless, fathomless, infinite; on the other hand, he becomes incarnated as Krishna in Hinduism, as Buddha in Buddhism, as Christ in Christianity. The intention is admirable enough: it is to account in some way for the existence of a spark of divinity in human life and to give that spark an intimate meaning. But, for our lives to have the meaning and purpose we require for them, is it necessary for us to confound ourselves with irrational descriptions of God? Is it necessary to try to make an uncreated creator out of God—or a cosmic satrap?

Will we slide into moral nihilism unless we think of the process of time as a predetermined plan existing first in the mind of God and then unfolding itself like a giant scroll before our eyes?

It has been the persistent habit of the traditional religions to shape their demands upon believers around a God who is responsible for everything that is and is to be. God, in the classic phraseology, is all-powerful, all-knowing, and everywhere present. The magnificent poetry of the Ninetieth Psalm contains the flowing description:

> Lord, thou hast been our dwelling-place in all generations.
> Before the mountains were brought forth,
> Or ever thou hadst formed the earth and the world,
> Even from everlasting to everlasting, thou art God.

God, in other words, *is* at the beginning of things, and in a position of active, conscious responsibility for everything.

A Unitarian Universalist does not shrink from recognizing that such a God is a staggering dilemma. If God is put at the beginning, as the creator of all things, the power responsible for all thing, he becomes a monstrous being! This, in truth, is what many sensitive spiritual geniuses have said about such a God all through the ages, from Zoroaster, to Voltaire, to William James, to Albert Schweitzer. A God who is responsible for everything is, at least in part, a god of violence, pain, misery, injustice, brutality, and darkness.

If, on the other hand, you try to apologize for this God, who has presumably produced a world at least half lost to the powers of darkness and death, by saying that he promises redemption for some persons in an eternal future, you are merely turning a brutal deity into a demented one. What would we think, for example, of a human father who deliberately tortures his children in the dark basement of his home, then turns around and lavishes favors on one of them while leaving the others to shiver and whimper? As shocking as such an act would be, it is infinitely less shocking than the behavior of a deity who is capable of condemning human beings to an eternity of torment for sins committed in the briefest of lifetimes in a world for which this same deity is avowedly responsible. Here is a savagely disproportionate system of punishment which is an insult not only to reason but to justice as well.

The daughter of one of my colleagues came home on the verge of tears because a playmate told her that if she was naughty God would send her to burn forever in Hell. She was reminded of the mild disciplines she experienced at home, when they were absolutely necessary, and was told that if Daddy and Mommy could be that gentle, how much more gentle God must be.

It is a reasonably good answer to a child, yet it begs the question. If God is really at the beginning of things, if God truly controls, then it is small wonder that he could shock Voltaire with the slaughter of the innocents of Lisbon. We can imagine what Voltaire would say about the God who permits his creatures to conceive of the crematories of Buchenwald, the atom bombing of Hiroshima, the extermination of Hungary's freedom fighters, and the murders in Birmingham, Alabama.

Neither faith nor reason can refuse to face such questions. If divine planning actually presides over all the occasions of human life, then God, from a human point of view, is part demon. By the same token, if God, from a human point of view, is truly a loving God, he cannot by any means be an all-powerful God. If he is an all-powerful God, responsible for all that happens, capable of heeding even the sparrow's fall, then he can hardly be a loving God.

It is just such thoughts as these that form some of our strongest bonds of liberal religious fellowship. We know that these thoughts are real and pertinent and searching. We know that they cannot be dismissed with pulpit platitudes and bromides. We draw together in common horror before those who speak of God as if he is some kind of cosmic "Big Brother" who will set everything right if we just put his name on enough coins, stamps, public buildings and schoolroom walls.

Unitarian Universalists share a realization that if this traditional deity is real, he is beyond comprehension. We are inclined, in this instance, to agree with Julius Penrose in Cozzens' novel *By Love Possessed* that theology is "the homage . . . nonsense pays to sense."

In what ways, then, do we characteristically look for solutions to the problem of God? There are three main lines of direction: God and man's search for himself; God and idealized reality; God and the search for purpose.

May the Inner and the Outer Man Be One

A pair of Harvard sociologists reported recently to the American Anthropological Association on a research project which indicates that religion springs more from fear and anger than from peace and love. This statement was made as a tentative summary of results from a series of tests seeking to determine what motivates people in their religious beliefs. The findings would seem to confirm what psychotherapists have long noted in treating persons whose emotional difficulties include a pronounced religious element. Mary McCarthy, in her *Memories of a Catholic Girlhood,* writes: "From what I have seen, I am driven to the conclusion that religion is only good for good people, and I do not mean this as a paradox, but simply as an observable fact. Only good people can afford to be religious. For others, it is too great a temptation—a temptation to the deadly sins of pride and anger, chiefly, but one might also add sloth. My Grandmother McCarthy, I am sure, would have been a better woman if she had been an atheist or an agnostic."

Religious beliefs may all too easily become weapons in

the hands of infantile adults, justifying and sanctifying what, from a psychological point of view, is hostile and fear-ridden behavior. For many of us the search for God is the search for self. If we find God too easily and in too stereotyped a form, we are likely to end with a none-too-admirable self. God can be the vehicle of immaturity.

Until the beginning of our present century, virtually all matters concerning the human psyche were referred to theologians and philosophers. In the late eighteenth century, for example, psychology was taught in the same departments at Harvard and Yale as "Angelology." Ancient Athens, with its deeper respect for psychological insights, turned to ethical philosophers for guidance. Thus, Socrates, in one of his infrequent prayers, gave this magnificent description of the modern goals of mental health and psychotherapy: "Beloved Pan, and all ye other gods that haunt this place, give me beauty in the inward soul, and may the inner and the outer man be at one."

Centuries later, Augustine, a person of many facets, developed a keen eye for psychological truths. He taught that a person finds himself only when he is able to penetrate deeply enough into his experience to unite the subjective and objective aspects of his life. It is also at this point, Augustine said, that a person finds God.

If we continue up the slopes of history to the nineteenth century, before the advent of Sigmund Freud, we find the most penetrating psychological insights being offered by Kierkegaard and Nietzsche, both philosophers and both intensely interested in religion. Contrary to a widespread impression of his work, it was Nietzsche who sensed more clearly than most that without corresponding advances in human character, technical progress could lead to ethical nihilism. In reaction against this grave danger, he wrote his dramatic parable of the madman who comes into a village asking, "Where is God?" The people laugh and answer that

God has emigrated or gone on a trip. The madman then cries: "I will tell you where God has gone. We have killed him, you and I. We have unchained this earth from its sun. God remains dead, and we have killed him." At this point the madman lapses into silence, gazing at the people. They, too, become silent, looking at him. Then he speaks his final words: "I come too early. This tremendous event is still on its way."

Nietzsche was issuing an indictment against a mechanization of life which crushes the self and the ethical sense. The "tremendous event . . . still on its way" was, as he accurately predicted, the onrushing fury of twentieth-century collectivism, with its transformation of man into an automaton, without heart or soul.

The developing science of psychology became itself a portion of the mechanistic tendency. Watson's behaviorism in the United States and Pavlov's conditioned-response experiments in Russia cannot be called premeditated attempts to dehumanize man, for their underlying purpose was to discover ways to release man from fear and hostility. But from these and similar efforts an attempt was made to construct a *total* psychological view of man based on mechanistic principles. The error was obvious. Man is never *just* a conditioned creature. He is never the *complete* captive of a chain of stimulus and response. Man transcends conditioning and exercises choice by virtue of his capacity for self-awareness. His margins of choice are limited—to this extent the mechanistic psychology is correct—but within such margins as he possesses, he finds the meaning of freedom and responsibility. Here, also, is the dwelling place of his religious yearnings and his quest to understand the purposes of his being.

Few psychologists today would be willing to classify themselves as mechanistic thinkers. The tide in psychology, as in all sciences, is toward a far more open view. This is not to say that the wider scientific horizons offer proof of a particular conception of God, as some fuzzy-minded religious spokesmen tirelessly proclaim. But it is now scientifically respectable to examine what, for many, has been a closed area, and to seek ideas of God that sustain and magnify the human sense of freedom and ethical responsibility.

The coming of Sigmund Freud, interestingly enough, helped to turn the search for God inward to the self. His work had a shattering effect on traditional understandings of faith and morals. He demonstrated that many of the real reasons for our behavior have little to do with conscious theological beliefs, but stem instead from wishes, fears, and past experiences of which we have no conscious awareness. With Freud's insights as guides, it was possible to demonstrate that pious behavior is often motivated more by repressed hate of self than by love of God. Freud hovers behind Mary McCarthy's astute observation that only people who are good to begin with should risk the temptation of becoming ardent religious believers.

The popularizing of Freud's theories sent waves of alarm through the minds of many sincere ethical and religious thinkers. Seemingly, a new type of choiceless determinism was being forced upon man, this time in the guise of unconscious drives and instincts. Freud himself argued that the Judeo-Christian conception of God was an extension of childish desires for protection.

Once again, however, the meanings suggested by Freud's pioneering work have been broadened by the last quarter-century's trend away from a mechanistic interpretation of science. Psychoanalytical thinkers, such as Jung, Adler, Rank, Horney, and Fromm, have built on Freud's discoveries and have used the fruits of his genius to achieve a deepened and more positive interest in the role of ethics and religion. It became possible to proclaim that ethics cannot be attained by being dishonest with oneself, and that the idea of God as a cosmic parent who will always take care of his children—

especially if they belong to the right church—*is* inadequate.
Freud's magnificent accomplishment, broadened by those
who came after him, puts fresh, new, vital meaning into
Socrates' prayer. The oneness of the inner and outer man, a
unity of the different levels with the self—these are the basis
for sound ethics and constructive religious beliefs.

Liberal religion has never been bothered by the alleged
"conflict" between psychology and religion. In fact, our interest in the psychological aspects of spiritual life has been so
marked that some of our friendly critics have jokingly referred
to us as "The Church of Freud, Scientist." To us, psychotherapy and psychoanalysis are not substitutes for religion,
but are excitingly useful techniques for helping to clear away
some of the debris of anxiety, guilt and hatred which keep
us from enlarging our precious margins of freedom. Our purpose is to arrive at ethical and religious beliefs which will be
most expressive of the genuine self and of the real situation
in which we live. Augustine said that a person finds God
when he finds himself. There is nothing in modern psychology which would compel anyone, in the name of science, to
dispute Augustine's contention. A concept of God emerging
from a unified, unblocked, fully functioning self bears its
own warrant. To plumb the levels of the unconscious is to
tap springs of insight, creativity, and energy beyond anything
most people are aware they possess. For many of us, discovery
of self is indeed, as Augustine suggested, the beginning of a
discovery of a personal concept of God.

If self-discovery results in greater self-affirmation, what happens to the traditional idea of dependence on God? This is
a serious issue, if for no other reason than that it divides
people into argumentative camps. From the evangelical side
come the old bromides about "What a Friend I Have in
Jesus" and "God will take care of you." From the brasher
advocates of psychological scientism we hear the warning to
depend on no one or nothing but one's self, or suffer the

consequences of permanent immaturity and crippled self-respect.

It is wise to rephrase the problem. How can we, on the one hand, resolve to be accountable for our own actions, develop and use our own powers, and be mindful that each person must take responsibility in the long run for the development of his own life; and, on the other hand, acknowledge that we exist in a world of "given" realities which are much weightier than we are no matter how faithfully we apply ourselves to high moral tasks?

When the question is asked in this manner, we can reasonably hope to demonstrate that truly creative people are those who affirm themselves and their talents to the fullest possible extent, but at the same time acknowledge their dependence on life's unmerited favors, forces, and circumstances. We might call this a Unitarian Universalist's principle of grace and self-assertion. Every person has resources of creativity for which he is starkly and relentlessly responsible. At the same time, every person lives in depths of circumstances over which he exercises little or no control. How we are to adjust ourselves to these twin aspects of reality is every man's basic religious challenge. If he can accept the "revealed" answers of one of the traditional theologies, and finds that by doing so he is able to keep growing, make fuller use of his own powers, and preserve his humility and capacity for awe and wonder, who would have the effrontery to challenge his solution? But, let us have no doubt that Freud was right in saying that the idea of God *can* be used for anything but constructive ethical and religious purposes. It can be the projection of infantile fear and self-contempt. By the same token, it is necessary for us to be reminded that a superficial skepticism, untempered by an abiding sense of the mysteries of which we are a part, *can* be an unwholesome spiritual arrogance no healthier than the dogmatic orthodoxies we reject.

Fortunately, there is a kind of pride in one's own powers, which goes hand in hand with humility, and it delineates liberal religion at its best. For lack of a better term, we can call it self-esteem: a willingness to assert, without guilt, our capacities for freedom, responsibility, and creativity, while affirming, without anxiety, our constant dependence on forces beyond ourselves. Never need we fear to assert ourselves as long as we are able to feel a proportionate awe in realizing that truth is always greater than we are. Indeed, the truth we do *not* know grows larger precisely as we are able to discover more truth. We are free to rejoice in the use of our talents, to exult in our abilities to feel, create, and grow, in proportion to our wonder at the vast mystery of grace which surrounds us. To esteem ourselves properly means that we esteem also the other people about us and the indescribable, immeasurable reality of which we are all a part. For many of us, God is this reality. Self-assertion and dependence are reconciled. The religious man and the psychologically healthy man become one.

To Find the Province of the Divine

Arthur Winner, the central figure in Cozzens' novel *By Love Possessed,* is musing about his father's religious views. The author consistently refers to Mr. Winner, Sr. as "The Man of Reason."

"In short," the lines read, "did the Man of Reason ever accept the story of the incarnate godhead, or the story of the risen Christ . . .? The Man of Reason had done the reading of his day and what was he being told (by his friend, the rector) but the very stuff of myth—the woman got with child by the deity in time to bear the infant savior at the winter solstice; the grievous formal murder of the theanthropus whose earth-breaking return from the dead must occur near the vernal equinox. Could the Man of Reason credit the dreadful drama's orthodox accounting-for? Could ethical as-

sent ever be given by him to all the shocking, the really
monstrous, dogma of the atonement implied? What was here
but allegorical fantasy, a laborious attempt in symbols to relate the finite known to the infinite unknown? You received
such stories, not as shedding light on, but as admitting, the
mystery awesome and permanent of life."

This is a familiar setting for Unitarian Universalists, who
also do the reading of their day and reflect upon their experience. They arrive where Arthur Winner, Sr. arrived,
with a sureness of feeling that the God whose substance can
be verified only by such tortuous dogmas as the atonement
is a God who sheds no light on the awesome and permanent
mysteries of life.

Then what does a person do? If he is an Arthur Winner,
Sr., he remains in the Episcopal Church, telling himself that
the stuff of this myth has long been the sacred fiction of his
people, a fable so honored that it has a vested right.

Another option is that claimed by those who seek the
province of the divine in precincts other than the ones established for the veneration of the ancient creeds and theologies.
They look for sustaining and satisfying intimations of God,
free from the clutter of inherited dogmas.

Such a one, for example, is Albert Schweitzer, who believes
that he has discovered and experienced God as ethical will
within himself. He contrasts this inner awareness with what
he calls knowledge of God from the world. The God who is
known through philosophy, says Schweitzer, is impersonal
Force; the God he experiences is ethical Will. They do not
coincide, Schweitzer admits. They are one, but how they are
one he does not understand. Here are his words: "The knowledge concerning God which is derived from nature is always
imperfect and inadequate, because we perceive the things
in the world from without only. I see the tree grow, and I
see it cover itself with leaves and blossoms; but I do not
understand the forces which effect this; their generative

power remains a mystery to me. In myself, on the other hand, I know things from within. The creative force which produces and sustains all that is, reveals itself in me in a way in which I do not get to know it elsewhere, namely, as ethical Will, as something which desires to be creative within me. This mystery, which I have experienced, is the decisive factor in my thinking, my willing and my understanding. My life is completely and unmistakably determined by the mysterious experience of God revealing Himself within me as ethical Will and desiring to take hold of my life." *

This is what Schweitzer calls his ethical mysticism. It is the apogee of a religious outlook cultivated by many of us. No claim is made that the old metaphysical problems are solved. The concern is with a private, overpowering experience of God's presence as a living, moral force in the individual life. No comprehensive effort is made to define God. There is no necessity for dogmas of incarnation or atonement. God is experienced in the inner man!

The advantage of such genuinely felt ethical mysticism is its universality. It is not a denominational or sectarian experience. The Hindu, Buddhist, Jewish, Moslem, Roman Catholic and Unitarian Universalist ethical mystics stand on common ground. But, since mysticism is capable of producing neurotics as well as saints, we are forced to conclude that it is not an end in itself. We can say, however, that it is one path to high religious experience and to a province of the divine against which reason and intelligence need not rebel. The test is mysticism's product.

In the powerful mind of Benedict Spinoza we make contact with still another approach to God which has captured the imagination of many religious liberals since this seventeenth-century genius set out to find an experience of God acceptable to people of reason, skepticism and ethical sen-

---

* *Christianity and the Religions of the World*, Henry Holt, p. 75 f.

sitivity. Spinoza began with nature and divided it into two parts. One part is the active, invisible, vital process of nature: its creative force. The other is the massive product of creative force: the tangible, individual items, modes, or forms such as trees, winds, waters, hills, fields, stones, flowers, mountains, animals and human beings. For Spinoza, God *as substance* is this first part of nature; and God *as extension* is the second part. God is the vital, creative process and force beneath and within all things. God is the universe and all that is in it!

Spinoza then asked what we mean when we speak of the help of God. He answered that the help of God means the fixed and unchangeable order of nature, or the chain of natural events. The universal laws of nature and the decrees of God are one and the same. To use Spinoza's words: "From the infinite nature of God, all things follow by the same necessity, and in the same way, as it follows from the nature of a triangle, from eternity to eternity, that its three angles are equal to two right angles."

What the laws of the triangle are to all triangles, God is to the world. Therefore, since the will of God and the laws of nature are one and the same, it follows that all events in human life, and outside it, are governed by dependable, invariable laws, and not by the whim of an autocrat seated in the heavens. Spinoza concludes that man's gravest error is to try to make God out to be a conscious creature like himself, with limited, changeable desires and purposes. Our problem of evil, in which we attempt to reconcile the ills of life with the presumed goodness of God, is a purely human problem having nothing to do with God. Spinoza chided his fellows for forgetting Job's lesson that God is beyond our human problems of good and evil. Good and evil are relative to human tastes and experiences. They have no meaning in the universe as a whole.

As to whether God is in any sense a person, Spinoza an-

swered no. If triangles could talk, they would describe God
as triangular. If circles could talk, they would describe God
as circular. If horses could talk, they would describe God as
horselike. It is natural but incorrect for man to ascribe his
own attributes to God.

The will of God, Spinoza continued, is the sum of all
causes and all laws. The intellect of God is the sum of all
mind. The mental and molecular processes which constitute the double reality of the universe—these, and their
causes, and their laws, are God. Because this is a lawful universe, we must apply a measured understanding to human
actions. As reason provides us with the perception of God behind the chaotic flux of things in the universe, so reason
enables us to discover law in the chaotic flux of human desires and purposes. The action of reason is human liberty,
and it is the only real freedom available to men. We are free
to the extent that we know and understand ourselves, our
fellows, and the world in which we live. Thus do we fortify
ourselves to bear both faces of fortune. God is not a capri-
cious personality, absorbed in the private affairs of his devotees, but the invariable, sustaining order of the universe.
The moral man, perceiving things through this eye of eternity, rises above a fitful yearning to identify his personal
pleasure and desires with God, and achieves a high serenity
of contemplation and ethical wisdom.

Little wonder that Spinoza is the prototype of many present-
day Unitarian Universalists. His was a lastingly impressive monument of brave faith in a magnificently credible
and impersonal God. The province of the divine discovered
by this inspired grinder of lenses plays a still vital role in the
making of the modern mind.

Of more recent grapplings with the problem of God, based
on rejection of orthodox theology and a desire to reconcile
reason with faith, one that strikes a responsive chord with
some of us is the cultivated speculation carried on by Lewis

Mumford, who shares with us a high regard for the spiritual-
izing function of religion.

Mumford conceives of religion as the reaction of man
in his wholeness to the whole that surrounds him. Instead
of abandoning religion because of a rejection of orthodoxy,
he calls for an enlargement of religion's scope. He thinks
that religion, in proper modern forms, is capable of reestab-
lishing man where he belongs in the scale of significance,
at the center of a universe he consciously embraces and
interprets. He believes that "without excessive pride, we
may still nourish the hope that one day man will discover
a more viable way than even the saints have yet found to
nourish and enlarge the province of the divine."

This is the spirit in which Mumford wrestles with the
problem of God. In good Kantian fashion he concludes that
reason will not sustain the traditional placement of God
at the beginning of things. When religion makes God the
creator and all-wise author of the universe, it must either
gloss over the evils of existence at the expense of truth,
or it must advocate belief in another principle—that of a
Devil or demonic power which challenges the creator's sovereignty and defiles his creation. There is no way out of
this dilemma, says Mumford, except through a revolution in
our *thinking* about God. He pays his respects to the great
mystics, but sees little value in mysticism as a general technique because it is so often a glorified device for escaping the
present evils and potential horrors of life.

Having suggested a revolution, Mumford has no choice
but to attempt one. He begins with the facts of human experience which in the past have been represented by the
symbols of the creator God opposed by a destroying Devil:
the one directed toward greater fulfillment of life, the other
bending its energies to ravage and disrupt. This, after all,
says Mumford, is a true-enough picture of life. Nature is
double-edged in its effect upon man, blessing him at one

moment and crushing him the next. The impersonal forces
in the universe do frequently seem to move in opposite directions. God is to be sought, therefore, not as an explanation
of what is contradictory in nature, but as what emerges from
a fuller development of the human person. In other words,
God is not at the beginning but at the end of the evolution-
ary enterprise. Rather than being all-powerful and everywhere present, God is but rarely found in human existence
and will not emerge into fuller presence except as man
matures to a higher level of life. So rare is the presence of
divinity in human affairs, that when it does appear in any
substantial concentration, it becames the core of a new view
of the world, as in the person of an Akhenaton, a Moses, a
Zoroaster, a Buddha, a Confucius, a Jesus. With the appearance of such a person, a whole society takes on a new shape
and reveals new possibilities in the conduct of life.

What Mumford offers is an evolving God rather than a
God who has existed always in an absolute and permanent
form. Mumford believes that only some such concept of an
evolving God is capable of interpreting human experience
in a scientific age, and of freeing the spirit of man for contemporary religious adventures. Faith, as he conceives it, is
the belief that there is a divine purpose which is still struggling into existence, even as man struggles for a higher life;
and that both, in spite of life's irrationalities, will finally
prevail: "If the universe, as the physicists now suppose, has
taken some three billion years to come forth out of chaos
and old night, God is the faint glimmer of a design still fully
to emerge, a rationality still to be achieved, a justice still to
be established, a love still to be fulfilled."

Through the use of unique, individual expressions such
as we find in the convictions of a Schweitzer, a Spinoza,
and a Mumford, I have attempted to sketch some of the
God concepts available to and held by various Unitarian
Universalists. Once again it is important to stress the range

of diversity not only permitted but encouraged in a fellowship of religious seekers.

Whatever Yields to Human Guidance

Finally, we turn our attention to still another approach
to man's relationship to life as a whole—an approach which
exercises great influence not only among us, but on thoughtful people the world around. It is religious Humanism.

In 1945, the Harvard University Press issued a volume entitled *Religion and Our Divided Denominations*. It was an
attempt to analyze the role of religious groups in serving
the cause of a unified, national life. The expected chapters
were there: Roman Catholicism, Protestantism, and Judaism.
There was also a section entitled "Humanism." Dean Wil-
lard L. Sperry, the editor, justified its inclusion with these
words: "The chapter on Humanism . . . is a recognition of
the fact that . . . there is a great body of persons . . . who are
idealists and loyal servants of their fellow man, but who find
themselves intellectually unable to profess . . . faith in God.
An English bishop has said that fifty percent of the intelligent
people of the modern world are humanists. These persons . . .
deserve recognition."

What is this Humanism, which an English bishop credits
with claiming the loyalty of half the world's intelligent people and which profoundly influences the religious thinking
of large numbers of Unitarian Universalists? Its roots are
deep in human soil. A millennium before the birth of Jesus,
the Aeolians, Dorians and Ionians swept into Greece from
the north, bearing their gods with them. For centuries, their
wise men wrestled with the task of adjusting these gods to a
new land and a new way of life. Their speculations became
steadily more obscure. Finally, some four hundred and fifty
years before the Christian era, a voice spoke in clear and open

protest against the unintelligible popular theology. It was
Protagoras, who said: "As for the Gods, I do not know
whether they exist or not. Life is too short for such difficult
enquiries. . . . Man is the measure of all things."

For his pains, Protagoras was banished from Greece. Seeking haven in Sicily, he was lost at sea. Inquisitors poked into
the corners and cupboards of the homeland, ferreting out
every copy of his books that could be found, and each was
burned in the public square. Nevertheless, Protagoras is
justly remembered as the first Humanist. His is still the classical definition of Humanism, an approach to thought and
action which assigns an overriding interest to the affairs of
men, as compared to the supernatural or the abstract. One
of the most memorable summaries of the Humanist faith is
Alexander Pope's:

> Know then thyself. Presume not God to scan;
> The proper study of mankind is man.

The late Dr. Charles E. Park, for many years the eloquent
and scholarly minister of Boston's First Church, described
the prophetic role of Humanism as ". . . a protest against un-
profitable speculation concerning matters which, by their
very nature, lie beyond the reach of man's comprehension;
and an appeal to philosophy to give the first freshness of its
vigor to problems that fall within its scope. It appears peri-
odically in the history of thought, to keep philosophy within
its proper bounds. When scribes, rabbis, and Pharisees in
Palestine could find nothing better to do than to get themselves all snarled up in useless conjectures as to the meaning
and scope of their precious Law, Jesus appeared teaching the
importance of considering the dignity of human nature, the
potential capabilities of the human spirit. . . ."

Did Dr. Park mean that Jesus was a Humanist? Certainly
not in the strict sense of the word, since Jesus did not hesitate

to "scan" God. What Dr. Park meant is that Jesus fulfilled the *spirit* of Humanism by demanding first consideration for the dignity of human nature. "We may call Jesus an unconscious Humanist," said Park, "for if you take away the humanistic element in his teachings there is little left." With equal fairness, we could say the same of Schweitzer, Spinoza and Mumford. Schweitzer finds God to be ethical Will within himself. What is ethical Will but a ringing affirmation of human dignity? Spinoza found God in the sum of all nature and all mind. What was the purpose of his quest but to confirm the moral capabilities of man? Mumford sees God as "the faint glimmer of a design still fully to emerge, a rationality still to be achieved, a justice still to be established, a love still to be fulfilled." How is this to come about? It must emerge, says Mumford, from "a fuller development of the human person." So these men of reason, though they presume to "scan" God, fulfill the spirit of Humanism. Man is the measure of their moral passion.

I make a point of this to dispel a confusion which arises from trying to build walls around Humanism and Theism to separate them sharply and distinctly from one another, as if a man can be faithful to the ideals of Humanism only by banishing God from his vocabulary, and vice versa. From time to time, in the past quarter of a century, tempers have frayed among Unitarian Universalists over the words Humanism and God. This can happen only when we forget what we are supposed to be: open-minded seekers after truth, each basically independent, each free to arrive at convictions without prejudice to his good standing, each deserving of respect for the integrity of his motives. *These* are our distinguishing characteristics, and not whether we choose to call ourselves Theists, Humanists, or something else.

There are two fundamental aspects of Humanism. The first is a religious attitude. The second is an approach to the nature of man.

The Humanist asks: Must religion be defined as man's relation to the supernatural? He unhesitatingly answers, no. The
object of religion, he says, is the integration and fulfillment
of man. It is commitment to finding and living the kind
of life that man's basic needs and aspiration make most compelling and desirable. Religion is not an *activity* separate
from other human activities. It is an *attitude* permeating all
activities. Thus, for the Humanist, the traditional understanding of religion as the binding of a man to a supernatural
order gives way to an appreciation of religion as the commitment of a man to those causes and ideals which seem to him
to have significance in the human quest for the good life.
Whatever God may eventually prove to be, there are now
obvious human needs to be satisfied, human friendships to
be cultivated, human loves to be fostered, physical and spiritual needs to be met. The highest purpose of religion is to
unite intelligence, compassion and technique to meet these
needs. To the late Dr. Curtis Reese, one of the most profound and persuasive of Unitarian Humanists, "... religion
is the natural functioning of a normal person in the effort
to achieve a full, a free and a socially useful life. ... As thus
understood, religion will wield an ever greater force in human affairs. Like art, it may consciously plan its remaking.
Like philosophy, it may devote time to speculative interests. Like government, it may try new social relationships. In
and through these phases of life and many others, religion
will grow greater through the years and those who commit
themselves to it will find the supreme adventure." *

By its very name, Humanism centers its attention on man
and on what can be called the "human situation." Traditional theology also has a doctrine of man, and "crisis" theologians speak often of the human situation. So, it is here
that we find a genuinely sharp conflict between Humanism
and orthodoxy. In orthodox doctrine, man's weakness stands

* *The Meaning of Humanism*, Beacon Press, p. 17.

in overwhelming contrast to God's infinite strength. Religion is God's revealed scheme for man's salvation, which man, in his essential corruption, cannot possibly achieve on his own. Humanism asserts that man can be thought of as essentially corrupt, not by comparison with God, but only by comparison with an imaginary perfect man, who has conquered every sin, vanquished every limitation, overcome every temptation, and solved every problem—a man, in brief, who never has and never will exist.

The Humanist approaches the condition of man from another direction. His outlook is something like that of the producers of certain adult TV westerns. In the old-fashioned "horse opera" there was no doubt about the distinction between good and evil. The good guys and the bad guys were acutely delineated. There were no mixed motives. The heroes were completely unselfish and noble, and the villains were completely evil and corrupt. The adventure thundered to a remorseless conclusion. That which was completely good would triumph. That which was completely bad would perish. In some of the TV versions of life among the sagebrush and stagecoaches, the heroes find themselves in situations of genuine moral complexity, where rights and wrongs are exasperatingly intermingled, motives are tangled, ethical distinctions are fuzzy, and morality is often gray in tone.

Humanism denies the completely separate existence in real life of good and evil. It contradicts orthodoxy's contrast of an all-perfect God with an all-corrupt man. Instead, the Humanist views man as a mixture of frictions, tensions, and shifting equilibriums. For the Humanist, man is potentially and essentially a "normal" creature. The purpose of religion is to help him to make the best possible use of his normality.

Most of us are familiar with the kind of public prayer which tells God of a number of matters about which, as all-knowing, he should already be well informed. It then goes on to ask God for favors, which, as all-powerful, he should already have given. A Humanist would reverse this procedure. He would not be inclined to offer God information he did not require, nor would he be likely to ask for more than had already been given. Instead, he would be likely to dwell on the sadness and humiliation he feels for the manner in which he, and others, leave largely untried the copious endowments already in human hands. The Humanist believes, in other words, that man is perfectly capable of finding within himself, and within the bounties of his environment, the resources with which he may satisfy his reasonable needs. An influential Humanist spokesman, Dr. J. A. C. F. Auer, describes this outlook with an old Dutch proverb: "Let each man row with the oars he has." He then goes on to explain: "As long as our explanation of man's real nature bears reference only to the saints who need solve problems no longer, or to irredeemable sinners who are constitutionally unable to solve any problems—as long as we refuse to pay attention to the norm which is found between these two, we shall get nowhere. As long as we judge man by his present performance, refusing to take into account a possible improvement resulting from a better use of his assets, we shall get nowhere." *

Humanism is the religious conviction that man *can* get somewhere, that he can improve, that he has within himself all the potential capacities he needs for solving the problems he can reasonably be expected to solve. Religion for the Humanist is primarily functional rather than speculative, and its function is to inspire and strengthen those attitudes which will bring man to the fullest possible consciousness of his freedom, his reason, his aesthetic depths, and his moral capabilities.

It may be that I love my Unitarian Universalist affiliation best of all because every congregation harbors a mixture of Theists and Humanists. They are, in my opinion, exceed-

* *Humanism Versus Theism*, Antioch Press, p. 27.

ingly good for one another. The Theist, whether of the
Schweitzer, Spinoza, or Mumford type (or some other), ex-
emplifies a persistence in the search for God which is by
no means lacking in fruitful results. As Dr. Park said:
"Gleams and flashes of insight do come to him from the surrounding darkness, and help to lighten man's way through
life's maze." The Humanist, meanwhile, keeps reminding us
that the more insistently we turn a keen, intelligent face
toward "the instant need of things," the sooner we shall
know the immense capacities of the human spirit.

Here I Stand

It would not be gracious to conclude this chapter without
giving some indication of my personal position. I will do it
briefly because the background for what I am about to say
has been amply explored in the preceding material.

Believing as I do in the essential probity of man and in
the power of human intelligence motivated by love, I am
in thorough sympathy with Humanism's personal and social
aims. I am, to this extent, a Humanist. I am not willing,
however, to abandon my search for, and my speculations
about, God. I use the word "God" sparingly, because I have
a deep dislike for the slovenly, undisciplined and monot-
onous way in which it is employed by pulpiteers, politicians,
and people generally. We happen to live in a time when attempts to "merchandise" God are sometimes indistinguish-
able from efforts to sell cereals.

I believe thoroughly in applying the experimental method
to theology as well as to physics, chemistry, and musical com-
position. Throughout the ages, questions about the existence
and nature of God have been answered with abstractions
made necessary by a limited theory of knowledge. Immobi-
lized by a long-standing dualism of the mind and its object,
thought could conceive of God only as an object separate

from self. Thus, God must be either a figment of the mind
or an essence beyond the reach of human knowledge. If God
is inaccessible to the mind, the religiously inclined person
seemingly has two logical paths open to him. He may become
a thoroughgoing Humanist, content with the principle that
God is, at present, unknown or unknowable. Or, confessing
the inability of philosophy to verify God's existence and
nature, he may seek a nonphilosophical experience of God
in the self, in nature, or in a revelation that transcends knowledge. This was Kant's response to philosophical frustration,
and it has been the basis of prevailing schools of theology
since his time.

The experimental approach to the inquiry centers itself
in the problem of human existence, and asks first of all about
the *nature* of God. It is impossible to answer this question
without exploring the history of religions, and from such an
examination it becomes clear that the lesser and greater gods
of all religions have been the life process itself, idealized and
personified. Every god is clothed in the habits and moral
codes of his worshippers, and invariably reflects the changes
which influence the customs, outlooks, and goals of his
people. The god is warlike when his followers are warlike;
the god is peaceful when his followers are peaceful; the god
is a monarch when his people live under a king; the god
rules by justice, mercy, and reason when his worshippers (as
among the men of the Enlightenment) espouse and promote
democratic ideals. Thus, God, at all times and in all places,
is the Spirit of a people as they interpret their existence. To
the extent that the world of humanity is held consciously
in mind, God is the Spirit of the world. In so far as the universe is consciously conceived as a unity, God is the Spirit
of the universe. When men are split into many isolated
groups, there are many gods. If these groups are not in conflict with one another, there is a tendency for each to recog-

nize and respect the gods of the others. When conflict arises, bringing political and moral tensions, it is normal for each group to view its own god as true and real and the others as spurious. As mankind's segments achieve a greater sense of unity, especially through commerce, art, science, and moral idealism, God emerges more truly as the God of a spiritual universe, encompassing all that lives. But, at root, God is conceived as the soul of communal values, the personification of ideals, the reality of life's truest forces and purposes.

The advantage of such a conception—to say nothing of its existential truth—is that philosophical frustrations about God's "existence" are no longer involved. If the world is a reality, then so is the God who is the living experience, in one form or another, of all people in the world. Whatever reality there is to the life of an individual, clan, metropolis, nation, or humanity, is imparted in kind and degree to God. I would grant at once that the total reality of God is greater than any individual's or group's experience of it to date, but I would insist that it is of the kind I have been describing.

God, to me, is the Spirit of a spiritual universe in which all life shares an associated and interdependent destiny. God is the personification of experience in this spiritual universe. God embraces the so-called material world in which the conditions and actions of living occur, but God is also the symmetry of intelligence and conduct to which humans aspire. God, in brief, is the glorious sum of the living process, in which I, as a person, live, strive, and die. God is the existence I share with all that is or is to be. God is Being, personified and idealized to the utmost limits of my spiritual insight and exertion. He is as genuine as my own nature, and as boundless as my most imaginative hopes for growth. With every deepening of my insight, every strengthening of my moral will, every expansion of my knowledge, God is better known to me, more reverently understood, more personally and profoundly experienced.

What the Unitarian-Universalist fellowship offers me is the opportunity to be utterly myself in matters of theological belief. When I use the word God, it is with the full understanding of my fellows that I speak from personal conviction and experience, and not from any desire to impose a presumed revelation upon the minds of others. By the same token, I not only speak as my conscience dictates, but I also *listen* to what others are saying with an eagerness that comes from wanting to catch the gleams and flashes of their intimations of spirit. Thus, in effect, does my knowledge of God increase.

SEVEN

WITH THEIR OWN EYES

Education is the leading human souls to what is best, and making what is best out of them; and these two objects are always attainable together, and by the same means; the training which makes men happiest in themselves also makes them most service- able to others.

JOHN RUSKIN, *Stones of Venice*

ONE of the happiest reasons I know for being a Unitarian Universalist is our work with children. Nothing in our religion is more exciting to me than our methods and princi- ples of religious education. A new kind of church school has come into being in our midst in which the *individual child,* rather than a Bible or catechism, is the center of the program.

We teach Bible courses as part of our curriculum, but only as they contribute to our comprehensive aim of introducing the child to the moral, social, and religious understandings he must have in order to live with ethical force in our demo- cratic and diverse society. Let me explain.

Some time ago, I was telephoned by a stranger who, with- out preliminaries, asked me whether "the Bible is God's own word, or just a bunch of fairy tales." Feeling that a minister's task is kindness even toward the belligerent, I answered in my most considerate manner that I believed the Bible to be neither God's own word nor a bunch of fairy tales. I could not tell at the point whether my caller was a partisan of the theory of divine inspiration or of the fairy tale hypothesis. I was reasonably certain, however, that he was a partisan for one or the other, and his next sentence was confirmation. "It's got to be one or the other," he said, providing semanticists with another classic example of the undistributed middle. "If it isn't God's word, then it's just a bunch of fairy tales!" This particular examiner of my theology turned out to be a "divine revelation" man, bent on rescuing my soul from insufferable heresies, but he might well have been a zealot of the other school.

In working with children, we recognize first of all that the Bible is not an "either-or" matter. We live in a complicated climate of opinion about the Bible. At one extreme are those who dismiss the Bible as a mess of mythical nonsense. On the same basis, they might also dismiss the Koran, the Bhavagavad Gita, Homer, and Shakespeare. These violent belittlers of the Bible are usually in revolt against orthodox religion and have momentarily lost their discriminating sense of judgment. For them the Bible is an emotion-laden symbol, just as it is for "true Biblical believers," only in this instance it is an icon to be smashed. To such extremists I can only say that, whether they like it or not, the Bible is a foundation stone of western civilization. It is a major source of our ideas, habits and attitudes. From it have come many of our laws, social institutions, morals and folkways. It is a factor in our lives to be reckoned with sensibly, rationally, feelingly, and intelligently. To reject it out of hand as a pack of fairy tales is to betray a massive ignorance of what the Bible really contains.

At the opposite extreme are those to whom the Bible is the "capital W" Word of "capital G" God, verbally inspired by God the Father, dictated by God the Holy Ghost, and revealing, without jot or tittle of error, *the* divine scheme of eternal salvation for human souls. From Genesis to Revelation, word for word, and line by line, the hand of divine perfection is present.

This view is filled with arrogance. Those who refuse to accept it are immediately labeled sinful and perverse. Yet, those who hold it generally know little or nothing of how the Bible actually came to be composed, or what its discoverable sources, cultural settings, and historical backgrounds are. Many "believers" are offended if anyone reminds them that the Bible they read is a translation, giving rise to the now somewhat threadbare legend of the man at the tent meeting who, in a moment of unrestrained fervor, cried out that if English was good enough for the Apostle Paul, it was good enough for him! Though they are unlikely to recognize it, Biblical fundamentalists resemble the fundamentalists of other religions. The Wahabite Moslem will defend to the death the notion that the Koran is but an earthly copy of a heavenly original, dictated directly by Allah's angel of revelation to the Prophet Mohammed.

Psychologically, there is a common bond among true believers of various kinds. They want to know, and they want to know without shadow of doubt or turning. They want assurance that their feet are firmly planted on the soil of certainty. Since they insist on knowing what, through ordinary thought processes, is difficult or impossible to know, and since thinking is at best a burdensome occupation, they are quick to assign supernatural qualities to a scripture, institution or dogma which, it is claimed, produces perfect explanations and absolute answers.

There are untold millions of such Biblical certainty-seekers among us, and their tastes are catered to with equal success by evangelists and the producers of multi-million dollar movie extravaganzas. Recently, even one of the most respectable of encyclopedias, apparently unable to resist the profit potential of current credulities, offered what it called "a wonderful new book, the Deluxe Edition of THE BIBLE IN PICTURES." Putting its reputation for sound scholarship squarely on the line, the encyclopedia company promised

Jesus "walking on the sea, stilling the storm . . . calling his friend Lazarus from the tomb." The full authority of the famous encyclopedia was thrown behind legend, myth, and miracle without the faintest hint that these are something quite different from history. The sales pitch gave Judaism no more status than that of a forerunner to Christianity. Only Roman Catholic and Protestant churchmen were used as consultants. Yet, the claim was boldly made that here was "a Bible for *all* religions" (italics mine). The unwary buyer was told that he could "see the events actually happening . . . see them occur . . . with satisfying realism." He could "know" the "authentic" Garden of Eden and Noah's Ark. He could possess "a perfect representation of life in Bible Times."

To those who have some knowledge of the Bible, and of the particular encyclopedia's past glories, this advertising broadside is a shocking sellout to the resurgent Biblical fundamentalism of our times. Happily, we are not alone in a concern for sound Biblical scholarship and understanding. Typical of the discriminating approach to be found in other denominations are the sentiments recently expressed by Dr. Harold A. Bosley, a distinguished liberal preacher of The Methodist Church, who said, ". . . our . . . wooden-headed way of handling the Bible is responsible for a biblically illiterate generation. At one time, this book was the symbol of infallible truth to most Protestant Christians. But that was half a century ago. Our thought about this symbol has undergone a radical change. Now the most a thoughtful student can claim for it is that it contains the deepest insights we have into man's search for God. . . . But the Bible as a book is far from infallible. It does not contain one theology; it contains many different theologies. Many Christians over the last two generations have refused to accept this revision of a hallowed symbol. They continue to believe 'I must believe all of it or none of it.' "

What has happened to bring about the changed attitude toward the Bible described by Dr. Bosley? What has happened to alter so dramatically the Unitarian Universal approach to Biblical teaching for children? The basic answers, of course, are scholarship and a revolutionized view of what constitutes religious "learning" for a child. For more than a century, scholars have devoted their lives to an intensive, scientific study of the Bible, to dissolve away the mists of superstition, and to learn always a little more of the truth about it. How many laymen are there who know the origin of the Bible's name? Actually, it is an English rendering of a Greek word describing the inner bark of a reed which was once used as paper. The plural of this word, *ta biblia,* was employed by early Greek-speaking Christians to characterize their revered writings and simply meant "the books." Later Latin translators, none too dependable in their scholarship, used the feminine singular in place of the neuter plural, and thus launched the erroneous impression that the Bible is a single, unified book.

In medieval times, scribes with a finer sense of propriety tried to correct the mistake by using another word, *bibliotheca,* which signifies a library. They were completely justified in the attempt, because the Bible is a *collection* of books, a library, which does not express a single theme, but treats a wide diversity of subject matters. For example, the gloomy, sophisticated, skeptical viewpoint of the author of Ecclesiastes clashes sharply with the cosmic optimism of Isaiah. They write of two different world views and two different sets of spiritual experiences. Existence is meaningless to one, full of meaning to the other. Yet, both occupy places of prominence in the same Bible. There is no need to puzzle over the explanation if we know that the books of this library were written over a period of a thousand years, by authors of widely divergent outlooks and goals. It is not unnatural

at all that the Book of Judges is quite unlike the Letter of
James in moral tone and attitude.

Another simple historical fact, known by surprisingly few,
is that the early Christians had no scriptures of their own.
There was, as yet, no New Testament; consequently there
was no "Old" Testament either. The first Christian Bible
was the Jewish Bible, the Torah, translated from Hebrew
into Greek. Christians of the first and second generation lived
in readiness for the return of Christ. Since the Messiah and
Savior was to mount his throne as visible ruler of the universe at any moment, there was little reason to add to the
existing holy books of the Jews. It was enough to tell and
retell the wonder stories of Jesus by word of mouth. When
congregations gathered for religious services, there would be
reading from the Septuagint (Jewish Scriptures in Greek
translation), with additional renderings of Paul's letters and
those of other apostles.

A fair summary of what scholarship tells us about the
Old Testament is that we are dealing with a wonderfully
diversified product of about one thousand years of religious
and cultural evolution. What emerges from a painstaking
dissection of Genesis, Exodus, Leviticus, Numbers and Deu-
teronomy is a patchwork accomplished by editors who combined primitive Hebrew folklore and myth with legendary
accounts of how the Hebrew tribes came into existence and
developed into a nation. There are ancient legal codes and
manuals of hygiene, early poems and battle songs, of which
the Song of Deborah is probably the oldest written material
in the Bible. All of this is woven by succeeding generations
of editors into an epic story.

The original authors of the myths, legends, traditions, and
histories are unknown. The later editors are unknown. We
do know, however, that the cutting and pasting process went
on for several hundred years. We also know that during this
period the Hebrew people emerged from primitive forms

of religion, such as animal sacrifice, to much more elevated ones, and that this advancement can be plainly traced through the Old Testament books. Some eight hundred years before the time of Jesus, there arose among the Hebrews those remarkable men known as the prophets. In all, the Old Testament contains a dozen small prophetic books, the much larger one of Isaiah (which is actually several books), and the two major works attributed to Jeremiah. By this time Hebrew religion had produced a minority viewpoint of inspired ethical idealism, of which the prophets were the formulators, leaders, and spokesmen. It is this development which gives the Old Testament its most noble and morally influential literature.

The collection of Hebrew scriptures, this library known as the Old Testament, was translated into Greek for the use of Greek-speaking Jewish communities scattered over the Mediterranean area. It was taken up by the early Christian churches and adopted as their own. In this manner it was subjected to the re-interpretations which made it over into a familiar segment of the Christian salvation story.

The years rolled on and the fervor about Christ's imminent return faded. There arose, understandably, a need for scriptures distinctive to Christianity. The churches were honeycombed with conflicts and disputes, and to settle these some written authority was required. Appeals were made to the letters of Paul and others. Interest in the deeds and teachings of Jesus was transformed into a demand for authoritative accounts. Unhappily for us, the earliest forms of these memoirs have been lost. They did, however, form the basis of what we do have: the Gospels of the New Testament. Still, we remain much in the dark, for original manuscripts of the Gospels have never come to light. We possess only relatively late translations and copies of material which was first written long after Jesus' lifetime. There are formidable problems of textual and historical interpretation.

What we do know is that three of the Gospels (Matthew, Mark and Luke) are based on two sources: a collection of the sayings of Jesus, which Matthew treats one way and Luke another; and an earlier form of Mark's Gospel. The Gospel of John is regarded by most scholars as less trustworthy from a historical point of view. It is probable that it was composed much later than the other three, without even the pretense of being an account of actual events. It is impossible to reconcile the Gospel of John with its counterparts.

Reverence for the collection of works now known as the New Testament steadily increased. But, there were also tensions in connection with it. Many of the church leaders were suspicious of books which might conceivably outstrip their personal authority, but, at the same time, the bishops, as they had come to be called, recognized their need for written works to support their power. The dilemma was solved by claiming that the added volumes were really a part of Sacred Scripture—a "New" Testament as distinguished from the "Old"—and that only the properly designated authorities of the Church could interpret them.

Even with so brief and sketchy an introduction as this, the question of whether the Bible is a book dictated by God becomes facetious. The Bible is replete with inaccuracies, inconsistencies, and errors, which should surprise no one in a great library accumulated over a millennium from numberless sources, authors, editors and copyists. Basically, it is a bit unfair to attribute this aggregate to God. The Bible was inspired bit by bit and part by part by the experiences people underwent over centuries. In this sense, scripture is still being written, and will continue to be written as long as there are men and women who are spiritually sensitive to what is happening to them and their world. How much better it is to accept the Judeo-Christian Bible for its uniqueness as a library of ancient human experience, and to know and love it for this, rather than to attach a superstitious veneration to

WITH THEIR OWN EYES   133

it. The inspiration of the real Bible is that of wisdom dis-
tilled from struggle, and insight gained from the hard evolution of human life. The Bible makes just claims upon us,
not in terms of divine authorship, but on the basis of the
everlasting quest for the good life and the assurance that man,
in his search for meaning and purpose, must progress from
lesser to larger truths.

We Unitarian Universalists use the Bible in our children's
program in what we consider to be a realistc manner. We encourage children to separate facts of history from mythical
and theological explanations. We urge them to approach the
Bible with complete candor, on the assumption that its books
were written by human beings basically like ourselves. We
are quite certain that the youngsters in many orthodox Sunday Schools are not actually becoming acquainted with the
Bible at all. At least they are not becoming acquainted with
it as it is. What they are learning turns out to be rather startling when examined. Children can only grasp what they
have the capacity to absorb and understand, and this is
limited by age level and development. No one would try to
teach the Bible to the family collie, even if she happens to be
as bright as Lassie. Yet, much of what is attempted in teaching the Bible to children is quite as fruitless, and for a very
obvious reason. The complex structure of the Bible is such
that it takes a reasonably mature background of human experience to cope with it. We do not expect a seven-year-old
to read and comprehend Shakespeare. The language of the
Bible is certainly no simpler than that of the Bard of Avon.

I spoke of the startling results from conventional Sunday
School Bible teaching. Let me illustrate. Recently, a group
of fifty college sophomores was selected on the basis of demonstrated scholastic aptitude and achievement. The students
had all been subjected as children to Bible training in either
orthodox Protestant or Catholic churches. They were then
given a five-week refresher course, followed by an examina-

tion which demonstrated that only eight or nine possessed
a trustworthy knowledge of the Bible. The rest were in a
state of marked confusion. They had no real conception of
the differences between the Old and New Testaments. Many
thought of Jesus as appearing in both. Some thought he gave
the Ten Commandments to Moses. A few remembered him
as the companion of Job. The sentiment was general that
everything in the Bible had happened at about the same time
and in the same locale. There was no awareness of a substantial difference in time between the period of Abraham
and the era of Paul. Most of the students thought of the Bible
as teaching a single, clear ethical code throughout. The majority, in spite of massive ignorance of its contents, insisted
that the Bible was to be accepted as a whole!

There were no marked differences between Protestant and
Roman Catholic students. Accuracy of Biblical knowledge
was lacking in approximately equal portions.

The only possible conclusion from this particular research
report, and it is borne out by other, similar studies, is that
teaching of the Bible *can* do more harm than good. Given
the approach generally used, it could not be otherwise. In
Unitarian Universalist Church Schools, Biblical materials are
used very sparingly with the younger children, not because
we want to deprive them of Biblical knowledge and inspiration, but because we want them to have a chance to know it
as it should be known. This can happen only at the upper
age levels when, unfortunately, many children stop going to
Sunday School! The cramming of indiscriminate Biblical
memorizations into the minds of small children achieves, as
with the fifty sophomores, the most scrambled results.

Small children have scant capacity for comprehending past
time. To a five-year-old, a thousand years ago is little different from yesterday. He lives and thinks in the present tense
for the obvious reason that he has not yet had an opportunity
to develop within himself a depth of memory. Would anyone

advise teaching a five-year-old the complexities of ancient
Greek history and philosophy? How can he be expected to
do any better with the history and philosophy of ancient
Palestine? No one can fit ideas of history into a pattern of
time until there has been a development of proportion and
sequence in the mind. It is the same with space. When we
were driving from Indiana to New Mexico, our son, then
four, insisted upon being briefed by road map as to where
we were. It was a hopelessly frustrating task. Terre Haute
and Tulsa were, as far as he was concerned, just outside
Indianapolis. He had not yet reached the mental age of
spatial sophistication. If, before reaching that age, we were
to try to fill his mind with Biblical places and events, we
would fasten on him the same jumble of misinformation
found in the fifty sophomores. What is created by premature
Bible teaching is premature mental chaos.

I have had the benefit of a good deal of postgraduate education in the literature of the Bible. My own earlier jumble
of misinformation has long since been unscrambled, so it
is not easy for me to imagine what the Biblical mind of a
youngster must be like after he has been exposed to a few
years of Sunday School. I suspect that one typical pattern
would be to believe that—just yesterday—a whitebearded
giant named God was telling a king to kill everybody except
his own relatives (the story of Samuel, Saul, and the Amale-
kites), and that at the same time God was also telling another
man to build a great ship in which to rescue his family and
two of each kind of animal (because God was going to drown
everyone else) and that there was a man named Jesus living
in the same place who taught that God loved everybody but
was still going to burn all the bad people. It is worth noting
that children are aware of the fact that they are often "bad."

My heart goes out to the youngsters who are currently
learning that the good Jesus and the savage David were both
faithful servants of God, and, at the same time, that the

tricky and dishonest Jacob was a favorite of God and was rewarded while the good Jesus was allowed to die on a cross; and that, just a few days ago, God slew all the first-born children of Egypt because the Egyptian king was quarreling with Moses.

Exaggerated as I make it sound, this is precisely the kind of problem we face when it comes to teaching the Bible to children. Most people have been taught that way and have never gotten over it! We are not in danger of repeating the error in Unitarian Universalist Church Schools, because we are concerned first of all with the individual child's learning development and not with a hasty administration of Biblical salvation. We want our children to know the Bible, but we are determined that they shall have the kind of knowledge they can later trust and respect. To five- and six-year-olds we introduce some of the simplest Bible stories, such as the Christmas legends, and some of the most familiar teachings, such as the Golden Rule. Then, with sevens or eights we use our first Bible storybook. It is the tale of Joseph, chosen because of its dramatic human interest as a family-centered saga of jealousy, achievement and forgiveness. In still another course, entitled "From Long Ago and Many Lands," we study forty-one stories of the religious myths and legends of many different peoples. Seven of these stories are from the Bible.

Our nines and tens learn the Bible stories of creation and have an opportunity to compare them with other ancient creation stories and with the modern scientific theories of how the universe was formed.

At age eleven, our youngsters begin their first serious probe of the life of Jesus. Teenagers are exposed to a survey of the historical drama of ancient Israel and a thorough study of Moses, interpreted through a study of the concept of law, and later become acquainted with the great prophets. High-schoolers are expected to dig deeper into the teachings of

Jesus, the beginnings of Christianity, and the development of the various Christian groups.

Please understand that I have been writing only of that portion of our program which deals specifically with Biblical materials. There is far, far more than the Bible in our program as a whole. The Bible, as it is customarily taught in Sunday School, is not in our opinion a *proper* book for small children. Our fundamental concern in religious education is that the child shall have a foundation of understanding, awakened interest, enriched experience, and tolerant curiosity to appreciate not only the Bible, when he is really capable of comprehending it, but many other founts of spiritual inspiration as well. If the foundation is not built first, the Bible, for all rational purposes, is wasted on a child.

The Great End in Religious Instruction

Traditional approaches to religious education rest on the notion that human nature is alienated from God, and can only be reunited by learning and accepting a doctrinal plan of salvation. Children, according to this older method, must be taught about a saving revelation which alone can rescue them from their "evil" selves, since they are incapable of accomplishing this for themselves.

Religious education in Unitarian Universalist churches is founded on the conviction that human nature, rather than alienating us from God, actually binds us to the universe, and to all that sustains it. The natural curiosities and urges of children, rather than being "wicked," are the very resources on which a program of religious education should be built. We offer every child a chance to achieve a religion of his own! If our boys and girls are to have a religion of their own, we must, in the Church Schools, do everything in our power to augment their experiences so that they may discover religion for themselves. "Thou shalt love thy neighbor as thyself." This is the type of injunction children have

been memorizing in Sunday Schools for generations. But if
the beginning premise is that the child is lost to start with
and can be saved only by conversion, grace, and unquestioning creedal belief, what possible meaning can the injunction
have? Actually, it is a plain statement of fact that you cannnot
love your neighbor effectively if you feel contempt for self,
if you cannot, dare not, and have not the freedom to trust
and respect yourself. Unless boys and girls are able to believe
that *they* are worth loving, there is no logic in expecting
them to learn how to love their neighbors. To help our children to build an awareness of their own worth, and thus to
create a genuine foundation for respecting the worth of
others, is one of our supreme aims in religious education—
from the nursery on. If anyone thinks that the nursery, with
its finger paints, crayons, clay, sand box, and picture books, is
no place to begin an education in religion, let him ponder
this report by Dr. Ernest Chave of a nursery conversation:
" 'Your parents are coming to see me tonight, and they will
want to know what you have been doing. What shall I tell
them?' asked the teacher. 'Tell them I'm learning to take
care of myself,' answered one child. 'I'm learning to paint,'
said another. 'Tell them I'm learning to fight,' shouted a
boy who, as an only child, was making more progress than
his words might indicate." * Each child expressed in his own
way the lesson of his own personal growth and sense of
worth. Yes, with an understanding teacher, religious education as an adventure and not as an ordeal *does* begin amidst
the clutter of a nursery room!

We believe that a child's religion grows out of normal experience. Religion is not something to be "given" to a child,
but something to be nurtured and encouraged in a child's
unfolding life. We believe that religion, if given a chance,
will grow naturally out of a child's everyday living and ma-

* *A Functional Approach to Religious Education*, University of Chicago Press,
p. 39.

turing, which is why we emphasize the enrichment of experiences in the here and now rather than confining ourselves exclusively to a rehearsal of the deeds of Jesus or other ancient Biblical heroes. We believe that young people are ready for direct, immediate experiences of wind, rain, sun, seeds, animals, birth, growth, and death. Out of the wonder of such experiences come the beginnings of religion. We believe that a primary order of business for a Church School is to help children to articulate such experiences in their own words, *before* their minds have been encased in adult explanations and reasonings. Instead of being taught to memorize traditional prayers or rituals—and then to repeat them parrotlike—small children should be given the freedom to speak of their awes, enthusiasms, fears, and questionings in their own unconstrained way. Heartening youngsters to search the stillnesses of their here-and-now experiences is to us the soundest beginning of a religion which will mature. The time will come—and they will be ready for it—when their own searchings can be profitably and excitingly compared to those of an Isaiah, a Jesus, a Paul, a Gandhi.

More than a century ago, William Ellery Channing did a remarkable job of formulating what has become *in fact* our general aim of religious education: "The great end in religious instruction ... is not to stamp our minds irresistibly on the young, but to stir up their own; not to make them see with our eyes, but to look inquiringly and steadily with their own; not to impose religion upon them in the form of arbitrary rules, which rest on no foundation but our own word and will, but to awaken the conscience, the moral discernment, so that they may discern and approve for themselves what is everlastingly right and good. . . ."

As a Unitarian Universalist I belong to a large and evergrowing group of parents who are determined to provide a religious education for children which is free from dogmatic, Bible-centered unrealities and confusions.

We encourage in children a *natural* development of religious faith based primarily on direct experience.

We avoid *imposing* religious beliefs of any kind.

We never suggest that an ideal is to be cherished *simply* because it is honored in our church or our religion.

We encourage a continual search to improve faith and life.

We do not teach a *finished* gospel.

We *expose* children to the thoughts and beliefs of many religions.

We do not teach that religious truth is to be found *only* in the Judeo-Christian Bible.

We heartily urge children to ask questions, express their doubts, and seek answers that are *personally* satisfying to them.

We do everything possible to avoid an atmosphere in which children might feel that their natural *curiosity* is being repressed.

This philosophy represents a tremendous change from traditional Sunday School techniques. It is, in fact, a revolution, and we are still in the midst of it. One of the first and most obvious needs of such a revolution is the availability of suitable books and materials for class use. In recognition of this, a special Curriculum and Worship Committee was organized several years ago, with Unitarian, Universalist, Ethical Society and Quaker representatives. Year by year, as a result of the committee's efforts, a new Beacon Series of nonsectarian, educationally sound religious curricula has emerged and expanded. For those who would like to know more about these materials, a pamphlet—*The New Beacon Series in Religious Education*—is available from the Division of Education, Unitarian Universalist Association, 25 Beacon Street, Boston 8, Massachusetts. It describes the contents of each book and gives additional information about liberal church school methods and practices.

Growth in our Church Schools has been explosive in recent years as more and more parents discover that there is a type of religious education available in which the child, rather than some set of adult doctrines, comes first. I would not want to pretend, however, that the discovery of Church Schools like ours is totally without disquieting confrontations.

Our children are not, cannot, and should not be quarantined from traditional religious ideas and credulities. They are bound to run into astonishing religious concepts among their playmates, to say nothing of some of the things they are likely to hear from grandparents, baby sitters, and certain overzealous public school teachers. This is an inevitable complication in guiding a child's religious development along liberal lines, but it is also an opportunity. In an extraordinary book entitled *The Questioning Child and Religion,** Edith F. Hunter tells how her four-year-old son, Graham, came running in from the yard, asking, "Mother, did Jesus get killed?" Mrs. Hunter was busy at the moment stirring a pudding on the stove. "Yes," she answered slowly, "Jesus did get killed."

"Why did he get killed?" Graham wanted to know. It was just before Good Friday. Something his playmates were discussing had puzzled the boy. Mrs. Hunter tried to arrange her thoughts, for she felt that her answer could well be the starting point of her son's grasp of the significance of Jesus' life. She was bothered because she suspected the subject was just a little too big for a four-year-old, but she wanted to give all the help she could.

"They killed Jesus," she answered carefully, "because some people did not like what he was teaching." Even as she spoke, she wondered what "teaching" would mean to Graham. He occasionally played school with his six-year-old sister, she as teacher. She taught him numbers and letters, which was all he knew about teaching. It would be confusing to him why

* Starr King Press, pp. 1-2.

anyone should be killed for that. But, there was something else that Graham wanted to know.

"But, Mother, how did they kill Jesus?"

Again she hesitated. "Well, they killed him in a way that they sometimes killed people in those days," she answered, hoping he would be satisfied.

"How?" Graham persisted, as the realization dawned in Mrs. Hunter that he had already heard from his playmates, but wanted verification from his mother.

"It was a cruel way. They put his body on a long board and stretched his arms out on another board that went across it, and stuck the whole thing in the ground."

"How did he stay up on it?" asked Graham.

"They put nails through his hands and feet," she replied, taking the pudding off the stove.

"Oh," he said and walked away.

As Mrs. Hunter explains, she had plans for her son's religious education, which did not include having him hear at the age of four about the crucifixion of Jesus. But he did hear about it, and she turned it into an opportunity for him to go as far with the subject as he wished to go at that moment. Graham's experience is not an isolated one. Our approach to religious education is radically at odds with the kind many of our children's playmates are receiving. In fact, it is the *other* kind of Sunday School training which our culture still takes for granted; and this places upon liberal religious parents an extra burden of responsibility. We must take *special* care to meet our children's needs for an interpretation of the situation in which they find themselves. We must relate our planned program of religious education to the plight which exists in our culture.

The process of developing a religion of one's own is slow, gradual, and a seven-day-a-week affair. Especially during a child's preschool years, a large part of this development must go on in the home. The direction it takes, its depth or lack

of depth, depends very largely on how seriously parents
assume their role as religious educators. It is impossible to
live with small children and not answer numerous questions
like Graham's each day. Because of this, we lay great stress
on parent participation in the church's program of religious
education.

Parents who think that they can put their children in Sunday School for an hour or two a week to "get" religious
education will not be comfortable in one of our churches.
Our program is designed to appeal to those who wish to
enter *with* their children upon an adventure in religious
growth.

Sophia L. Fahs has done more than any other individual to
inspire the kind of religious education I have been describing. Writing in the December, 1958, issue of *Parents' Magazine,* with my colleague, Harry B. Scholefield, she said:
"Parenthood is a combination of very serious responsibilities and utterly delightful opportunities. Parents watching
their children mature, each in his own way, know the
wisdom of the ancient Chinese philosopher. Asked what he
thought was the most precious experience in life, he replied:
'It is to hear a little child go down the road singing after
she has asked me the way.'"

Ernest W. Kuebler, former head of the Educational Division serving Unitarian Universalist churches, spoke for all
who are devoted to our kind of religious education when he
wrote: "The conditions that make for mankind's progress
are fundamentally ethical and religious. We want education
in religion to be education in universal religious values that
are discovered through personal experience and insights and
applicable to the world today."

EIGHT

WHAT A FEW CAN DO

We learn looking backward. We live looking forward.

ANONYMOUS

WHY are you doing this?" The year was 1947 and the questioner was dean of the faculty of the medical school in Vienna. The war was over, but its gruesome mementos were everywhere to be seen. We were sitting in a three-hundred-year-old room of Vienna's central hospital. The day's surgery and seminar sessions were ended. I was there as secretary to a team of prominent American physicians sponsored by the Unitarian Service Committee. Our purpose was to do all we could to provide Austrian doctors with the latest techniques of medicine and surgery. The once-proud center of the healing arts had suffered terribly from the ravages of Nazism and battle, and with the full cooperation of the newly established democratic government of Austria, the World Health Organization, and the four-power military occupation, the Unitarian Service Committee had organized a mission of twelve U. S. specialists to act as midwives at the rebirth of Austrian medicine. "Why are you doing this?" the dean asked.

Previously he had quizzed me about the religious interests of the twelve team members. His eyebrows lifted noticeably when I told him that only two of the American doctors were Unitarians, and that quite by happenstance. "Do you expect to gain Unitarian converts by this program?" he wanted to know. I told him that we had no desire but to do something useful for Austria. The work of the Unitarian Service Committee, I explained, was entirely nonsectarian. "Why are you doing this?" he inquired.

For most Unitarian Universalists, religion would mean little if it did not include enlightened conscience in action. Yet, we are not missionary-minded. By deliberate choice we send no missionaries over the face of the earth to convert others to our way of believing. In fact, as I have previously explained, we generally feel that people of other religions have as much to teach us as we have to teach them.

We have a moral equivalent for missionary activities. Kindled by compassionate imagination and fanned by a desire to share skills, resources, and goodwill with people the world around, the impulse to serve is mobilized in the *Unitarian Universalist Service Committee.*

Established in 1940 to aid refugees from Nazi Europe, the UUSC has kept pace with the changing needs of our changing times. There have been innumerable, dramatic, short-term relief operations, such as those involving homeless, hungry derelicts in Portugal, the postwar "cave children" of Naples, and Hungarian refugees of the heroic "Freedom Fighter" uprising. There have been years of rushing tons upon tons of food and assorted apparel to emergency areas in Europe and Asia. At the present time, typical UUSC programs include:

A Village Development and Training Project in the Nigerian community of Awo Omamma. The UUSC has purchased and sent numerous pieces of equipment and machinery to be used in constructing water tanks, demonstration housing, and the first secondary school in the area. A native Nigerian, a graduate of American universities, was the first member of a field staff later being augmented to include trained workers in health, nutrition and agriculture.

The Green House on the banks of the Arroyo in Gallup, New Mexico, where the Navaho people are cooperating with UUSC in a large-scale program emphasizing citizenship education, individual rehabilitation, family recreation, nursery education, and study of alcoholism. In addition to the year-round staff and activities, a special feature is a summer work-camp for Indian and non-Indian young people of college age, who work under supervision to help maintain the center's facilities and to take part in an extension recreation program with Navahos out on the reservation.

A Human Relations Council in Atlanta, Georgia, where a UUSC field representative is assigned to aid the Council to prepare and carry out a program of community education in preparation for and in connection with the desegregation of local schools.

There are many other projects as deserving of mention, but they are all characteristic of our conviction, as expressed through the UUSC, that people would rather be helped to stand on their own two feet than accept a handout. Whether they live in a teeming city or in a jungle village, no matter what their color, culture, or previous education, people prefer to take encouragement and training from a nonsectarian rather than a proselytizing agency.

To the Austrian dean, and to all others, I can only say that we support the Unitarian Universalist Service Committee because it represents our partnership with people—whoever and wherever they may be—with whom we can enter into a mutually helpful relationship. We become more self-reliant and self-respecting by helping others to do likewise. We do not expect anyone to pat us on the head for being "good," and we do not expect anyone to become converted in return for our interest. We work *with* and not *for* people. If it is possible for us to bring help, or know-how, or whatever, where it is needed, we want to try to meet the need; but only in keeping with what others, themselves, express as their desires. We never try to superimpose a project of our devising upon unwilling recipients.

We have consistently tried to adjust our program to changing patterns in the world. We try sincerely not to succumb to the temptation to tell people what they ought to be doing. Our ability to work is severely limited by the funds made available by voluntary contributions, so it is of the utmost importance that we choose wisely among the overwhelming needs to be found in an age of revolutionary change and disruption. From various vantage points, the UUSC has watched the attempts of Communism to wean men's minds and hearts away from any trust in the Western World. We have learned the dangers and pitfalls of entering into a tug of war for the affections of people on the basis of who offers the better handouts. Our projects are never conceived as competitions with Communism, any more than they are conceived as bringing the "light" of salvation to the heathen. We only wish to aid people to realize their own potentialities. By so doing we feel that we are demonstrating to ourselves that religion is far more than a Sunday morning gesture to God. Behind the UUSC there is a religious motive, but it is *not* the motive of seeking converts. It *is* the motive of demonstrating that good deeds lead the way to One World, One Humanity.

Strength and Promise

I have no argument with the great days of prayer organized by various church bodies. I am not inclined personally to enter into these efforts, but my feeling of respect for those who would pray us out of our difficulties comes under the heading of what might be called *reverence for reverence*. My own view of reality is that the world of human affairs is the world we make, and that there is no conscious intervention by a Will which exists outside human hearts and minds. That other persons see reality differently, and accept the possibility

that a personal God can intervene, does not in itself alarm
or disturb me. The religious life does not require uniformity. What it does require is that every honest person should
rethink the implications of his faith, take a look again and
again at his working hypotheses, and try to find ways of trans-
lating his own religious idiom into that of any other equally
honest person.

It may well be that in ways quite unknown to me the
unified prayers of hundreds of thousands are heard in some
fashion in the universe and do influence the course of human
events. At the very least, the act of praying has some effect
upon those who sincerely and deeply accept its reality. Behind our differences of approach stand the common problems. Human life is lived in a constantly shifting flux of
grandeur and horror, security and terror, amity and hostility.

As a nation we are the greatest example the world has
ever known of the affluent society: with the greatest plenty,
the most widely distributed possessions, the highest standard
of living people have ever experienced. And yet, Western
civilization, of which we are the professed leaders, brought
blood and anguish upon our century in the form of two
unprecedented world wars. And once again, in the midst of
our technological millennium, we walk daily on the brink of
a catastrophe so great that we can hardly grasp its possible
consequences. Nor is the threat of war a unique symptom
of distress in an otherwise gay and carefree world. The economic achievements we prize so highly are mocked by slums,
soaring crime rates, and racial violence. In the world at large,
the distribution of wealth is so inequitable that thoughtful
people are haunted by the fear of the consequences.

The point I most want to make about these evils is that
while we generally deplore them, we quite consistently refuse to recognize our responsibility for them, telling ourselves
instead that it is the wicked who are accountable. In World
War I it was Kaiser Wilhelm and the Huns. Later it was

Hitler, Mussolini, Tojo, and Stalin. Hitler, of course, blamed it all on the Jews. Today it is blamed on the Communists, who include, if the John Birch Society is heeded, the Chief Justice of the Supreme Court of the United States. Some blame it on Walter Reuther, others on the "munitions lobby," others on sinful human nature, and still others on "deluded do-gooders." Most of us badly want to believe in some sort of devil who is *really* responsible for the evils which beset us.

Religious fundamentalists have the advantage of being able to blame the *real* devil. The American Legion can blame the Civil Liberties Union.

We Unitarian Universalists, if we are true to conscience and reason, must be content with the hard fact that we, individually and collectively, create by our own practices the kind of world in which we live and suffer or rejoice. We know that no class, no group, no political party, no economic system, no dictators, no rebels, no religion can be either absolved from responsibility or singled out as the primary villain. So, if we were to fall down on our knees and pray "Oh God, bring peace to our world by helping us to realize that it is *we* who must wage peace: by our thoughts, by our acts, by our attitudes," we could utter such a prayer with a clear conscience.

Because humans are human and love to blame devils for their difficulties, religions are often sadly ineffective against the world's ills, though this is by no means an inherent or fatal flaw in the nature of religion itself. There is in religion a high tradition concerned with the *all* of life and dedicated to its enhancement. The great Hebrew prophets insisted that God's concern is with the well-being of *all* peoples. One of the finest sayings attributed to Jesus has him teaching: "But whosoever would be great among you, shall be your helper; and whosoever would be first among you, shall be servant of all." This principle is applicable to all human relations:

of parents and children, teachers and pupils, employers and
employees, privileged and underprivileged, nations and other
nations. Whenever religion fails, it fails not because of
an internal defect, but because religion is lived in people.
With people, profession of belief is never a substitute for
responsibility.

Back in 1939 a group of scholars, including physical scientists, social scientists, philosophers, and theologians of several
faiths, drew together in New York. They were stirred by the
specter of Nazism, but recognized it as a symptom of a
chronic illness of the century rather than the disease itself.
They hoped that together they might succeed in clarifying
moral problems. About once a year since, these scholars have
met. Some are agnostic; some frankly atheistic; others devout. For a long time their discussions were badly snarled in
contentions. There were frequent outbursts and angry arguments as one type of mind and experience clashed with another, but gradually they arrived at an astonishingly simple
conclusion: the crux of their concern can be summed up in a
single word—*responsibility*.

Religion may be a matter of prayer, but prayer without
responsibility is a mockery. Religious faith may at times be
a necessary retreat from the world, but retreat without a
vigorous return to responsibility is contempt for life.

When Little Rock was in the midst of its racial tensions
over Central High School, a Harvard social psychologist went
to see what the ministers of religion were doing about the
problem. There were only six who had risked their all by
calling upon their congregations to support the Supreme
Court decision. Four of them had already been fired and the
other two were expecting the axe momentarily. A second
and somewhat larger group consisted of the men who were
pastors of the more prominent and influential churches in
town. Although most of them personally favored integration,
they felt that they had to keep silent in order to preserve

the unity of their congregations. The third and largest group
was made up of men who, again for the most part, personally
favored integration but who dealt with the problem, as they
phrased it, "by praying for guidance." The psychologist concluded after talking with these men that what they seemed
to mean by praying for guidance was finding some way to
say something *without being heard.*

Believe me when I say that I do not stand in judgment on
these men. I am reasonably certain that I would not be found
in this third group. But, without actually being in the situation and having to make the concrete decision about my
personal course, I cannot say with positive assurance whether
I would take my stand with the first group or the second. I
can only say where I *hope* I would be found. Those of us
who would defend religion by relating it effectively to the
problems and conditions of life know that the ultimate test
is responsibility, from which there is no escape when greater
and lesser values are in conflict. We know that in order to
win a hearing for a reasonable and worthy concept of religion
there is no way of avoiding the sharp edges of choice.

The dismal showing so often made by religious spokesmen
and organized religious groups can be largely attributed, in
my opinion, to the narrow notion that religion is a system
of props and supports for the individual. Actually, I do not
contest that this is one of religion's significant and powerful
functions. Few of us can do without spiritual support and
solace, but a religious expression which turns only inward
upon itself, which fails to help us face and carry through
the moral responsibilities inherent in the economic, political,
and social structure of the world, is in decay. Religion's high
tradition as an instrument of deepening social conscience is
brought to shame if a church's primary attentions are focused
on rituals, fish frys, raffles, and conformity to convention.
History honors only those religionists who, from the depths
of their faith and conviction, cry out against economic and

social evils, paint a glowing picture of life as it should be when it is lived in mutual respect and service, and exalt the earth as a sacred trust for all.

Hearing this, someone is bound to say: "But wait. What can a mere handful do in a world like ours? On many issues we can't even agree among ourselves. How can we expect to do more than learn to live with all the grace and resignation we can muster?"

Unitarian Universalists *are* a mere handful. Though our adult church membership has doubled in the past decade, we are still only 153,000 or so in a huge sea of religious orthodoxy. Children enrolled in our Church Schools have tripled in number in ten years, yet they are a tiny segment of the nation's whole. With each passing month our graph line of growth continues to climb, but we are still talking of exceedingly modest totals in comparison with the overpowering statistics of other major religious bodies. Organized groups are now to be found in a thousand cities and towns from ocean to ocean, from Alaska to Panama City, whereas in 1947 our yearbook could list only 325 locations in the United States and Canada with Unitarian churches. Still, this is nothing, numerically, when compared with the Methodists, Baptists, or Roman Catholics.

In a mere handful, however, is the power to move mountains, conquer dread diseases, and *change the climate of a community*. A few years ago when a Unitarian minister was ordained in a southern city, a Jewish rabbi remarked to a friend: "I prefer to serve synagogues located in cities where there is a Unitarian Church because this institution has a cleansing effect upon a community." He might well have been thinking of the fact that from so small an acorn has grown such an amazing oak. Unitarian occupants of the White House have included John Adams, John Quincy Adams, Thomas Jefferson, Millard Fillmore and William Howard Taft. Calhoun, Webster, Sumner and Marshall were

Unitarian laymen. Seventeen of the seventy-seven Olympians in the Hall of Fame were Unitarians.

Impressive indeed is the roll of past literary figures: the Longfellows, Oliver Wendell Holmes, Ralph Cullen Bryant, Edward Everett Hale, Ralph Waldo Emerson, James Russell Lowell, Nathaniel Hawthorne, Bret Harte, Louisa May Alcott. Nor should we forget great historians such as George Bancroft, John Lothrop Morley, Francis Parkman, and William Prescott.

Because of our historical emphasis on service, our movement has produced an amazing number of pioneers in social, humanitarian, and educational fields. Championing the cause of women's right were Lucy Stone, Julia Ward Howe, Elizabeth Stanton, Susan B. Anthony and Margaret Fuller. In education some of the familiar names are those of Horace Mann, initiator of universal, nonsectarian, public education; Elizabeth Peabody, first American to establish a kindergarten; Cyrus Pierce, pioneer crusader for teacher training schools; and Peter Cooper, founder of the famed Cooper Union in New York City.

We would also include among the most honored of humanitarians: Dorothea Dix, whose boundless determination launched the reform movements in prisons, charity institutions and mental hospitals, and Dr. Samuel G. Howe, who founded the first school for the blind; Henry Bergh, creator of the Society for the Prevention of Cruelty to Children and founder of the Society for the Prevention of Cruelty to Animals. Others who have made outstanding application of their religious ideals to public welfare include George William Curtis, pioneer advocate of civil service, and Henry Bellows, originator of the United States Sanitary Commission, which later became the Red Cross.

Typical thinkers who laid the foundations of modern science were Isaac Newton, Joseph Priestley, Charles Darwin, Louis Agassiz, and Charles P. Steinmetz.

These representative leaders of the past are but a few of the many who justify the pride Unitarian Universalists understandably feel in the influence our religious movement has exerted. It has been all out of proportion to our numbers in molding public opinion, initiating social reform, and making history. Fortunately we can turn to the present with comparable satisfaction to find a brilliant array of leaders acting as spokesmen and exemplars of our way of life.

In public affairs and government there are such figures as Adlai Stevenson, Percival Brundage, James Killian, Chester Bowles, Sinclair Weeks, Justice Harold Burton, Theodore Sorensen and Senators Clark, Cotton, Douglas, Hruska, and Saltonstall. Among the giants of twentieth-century fine arts and literature are such representative figures as Frank Lloyd Wright, Bela Bartok, J. P. Marquand, and Fabian Bachrach. In education we claim such leaders as Harry D. Gideonse, Nils Y. Wessell, George D. Stoddard, Arthur E. Morgan, Reuben G. Gustavson, and Ernest B. MacNaughton. Unitarian historians include Henry Steele Commager, Dexter Perkins, and Arthur M. Schlesinger, Jr. Typical names of Unitarian Universalists among the top social scientists are Alfred McClung Lee, David Riesman, Thomas Dawes Eliot, and Ashley Montagu. In the various physical sciences and healing arts the list of distinguished names is so extensive it is unjust to single out a few.

The strength of Unitarian Universalism is the strength of those who, though they be but a handful, are determined not to let the complexities of life deaden the imagination. The promise of our faith is perhaps best summarized in the aspiration: "Give me the serenity to accept what cannot be changed, the courage to change what can be changed, and the wisdom to know one from the other." We seek constantly for confirmation of the moral might of the few.

As a practical example I would direct your attention to the Unitarian congregation I served so happily in Indianapolis. In February, 1959, we moved our entire congregation from a lovely but inadequate Tudor edifice into a glowing new contemporary structure. The final service in the old building, which had housed the congregation for half a century, was a deeply emotional experience. In my sermon I reminded the people that we took our heritage with us to the new location. A heritage is in people; in their memories, their inspirations, their hopes. Wherever the congregation is, there will its heritage be. I pointed out that the Indianapolis Unitarian heritage was crystallized in certain meaningful symbols which we would physically carry to the new building. There were the portrait heads of Ralph Waldo Emerson and Thomas Paine, representing the fine spiritual balance for which the congregation strived: Paine, the man of action and urgent devotion to political and religious freedom, the gadfly, the tireless worker whose worship was expended energy, whose energy was service, and whose service was boundless; Emerson, America's Socrates, who loved the quiet recesses of thought beneath the surfaces of life, found rationality and hope in the awakened mind, and bathed his soul in naturalistic mysticism. Here were two wondrous symbols of the concrete ends and goals of a liberal religious movement.

There was also the pulpit Bible of Edward Everett Hale. Everyone knows Hale as the author of *The Man Without a Country*. Not everyone remembers his brilliant career as a Unitarian minister. But, exceptionally lustrous it was, in spite of one of the archest examples of a clouded crystal ball known to our denomination. When Hale was a young man, fresh out of the Harvard Divinity School, he journeyed across the prairies to Des Moines, Iowa, as a candidate for the Des Moines Unitarian pulpit. The committee wrote back to Boston that they declined to issue a call to Mr. Hale because they considered him to be a young man of no promise. Hale returned to Boston and fashioned a fabulous career anyway, in the course of which he befriended a young minister named

Frank Scott Corey Wicks, who later went to Indianapolis to begin a forty-year stint as Unitarian prophet to the Hoosiers. In Hale's declining years he bequeathed his pulpit Bible to Frank Wicks, and thus it became a treasured possession of the Indianapolis church. That Bible, I told the congregation, symbolized the memorable years of Frank Wicks's labors for beauty, truth and goodness in Indiana.

Along with the Bible was the carefully recorded history of the Indianapolis congregation, into which we could dip to find such stories as the happenings in 1912 to Dr. Alembert Brayton, a devoted member of the Indianapolis church. A leper had been discovered in a remote section of the city—an aged, penniless, Negro widow. The city was horrified. A high board fence was built around that hovel that housed the woman and her daughter. No one would go near the place, no one that is but Dr. Brayton. He went every other day to sit with the woman and to reassure her as best he could. The patient had no money; she was hopelessly ill; and there was nothing medicine could do for her. She was ignorant, and her malady made her anything but an attractive companion. Dr. Brayton lost practice because other patients were afraid he would transmit the disease to them, but he had assumed a responsibility and he stuck to it. As the end approached, the leprous woman became more apprehensive. She begged the doctor to promise that he would be with her, as she put it, when she was "a-passin' over." He promised. Finally she sent for him. He stayed for hours. She asked him if he would sing the hymn "Lead, Kindly Light." Without benefit of an orthodox church background, he did not know the words, but the daughter dug out an old hymnbook. His friends always claimed he couldn't carry a tune in a bushel basket, but he sang as best he could. He sang his patient peacefully out of her suffering.

If there is a better example of the spirit of a congregation's heritage, it would not be easy to find. I told the Indianapolis

WHAT A FEW CAN DO   157

Unitarians that this was the kind of history they were taking
with them. In moving, I said, it would be well for us to look
out at the surrounding city and remember how much of
what made it civilized grew out of the vision and effort of
people who sat in the pews they occupied, or stood behind
the pulpit. There were the Marion County Juvenile Court,
the Boy's Club, the Day Nursery, the Cooperative Play-
schools, the Visiting Nurses Association, the Public Parks
Department, the Health and Welfare Council, the Girl
Scouts, the Planned Parenthood Association, the Civic Thea-
tre, the Civil Liberties Union, the Indianapolis Symphony,
the League of Women Voters. Each and every one of these
organizations traced its origin, at least in part, to the energies
of Indianapolis Unitarians. This is the power of the handful,
the strength of a few, when religion is wedded to responsibility, when a religious center faces outward toward its
civic circumference.

Today the Indiana Association for Mental Health is a
model of strength and effective service. Its programs in behalf of the mentally ill have attracted national attention and
are widely copied. It has transformed Indiana from one of
the most backward to one of the most advanced of states in
the prevention, care, treatment, and rehabilitation of disturbed minds. Fifteen years ago this same Association was on
the verge of bankruptcy and dissolution. With the leadership
of Dr. E. Burdette Backus, my predecessor in the Indianapolis Unitarian pulpit, and using the Unitarian church
building as a stopgap, rent-free headquarters, a handful kept
the Association alive, nurtured it back to health, rebuilt its
program, and set it on the path to national leadership.

On Halloween, thousands of children, representing scores
of churches and synagogues, haunt the streets of Indianapolis
as ghosts, goblins, and gremlins, sharing their "trick or treat"
with far less fortunate youngsters all over the world by col-
lecting pennies, nickels and dimes for UNICEF, the United

Nations Children's Fund. A few years ago, Unitarian Universalist children were the first and *only* ones in the entire city who participated in the program. A handful, yes, but a handful which has swelled to a cityful.

The present sponsor of the UNICEF Trick or Treat is the Indianapolis Council on World Affairs. A few years ago there was no such council in the city, and there probably would not be today if a handful, using the Unitarian church as a meeting place, had been unwilling to take the time and the trouble to hammer at the hard realities of getting such an organization under way. The Council is now one of the most vigorous, vital, and enlightening institutions in the community, and it makes a substantial difference in the Indianapolis cultural climate.

For two years the Indianapolis Mayor's Commission on Human Rights fought a lonely and thoroughly frustrating battle for a budget to carry out the assignments given to it by law. Finally the quest was crowned with success. Why? Because a handful—chiefly the members of the Human Relations Committee of the Unitarian Church—decided to do something about it. A telephone committee sprang into action, mobilizing persuasive pressures on the City Council. A hearing was attended by large numbers of citizens who had been alerted by the committee. The City Council voted a budget which gives Indianapolis an opportunity to draw abreast of other, similar communities in attempting to reduce intergroup tensions through professionally guided planning.

Religion Must Be Acted Out

I have used Indianapolis as a specific example because I know the situation intimately and at first hand. Hundreds of other communities could be chosen and examined with similar results. Virtually every Unitarian Universalist minister could duplicate out of his personal experience the story I have told about the Hoosier capital. A few who think clearly and intelligently, and who feel deeply their spiritual responsibility, possess influence vastly out of proportion to their numbers. In whatever concrete ways we may decide to exercise the power of the handful, the vital matter is to remember the foundations on which that power rests:

First, that religion is concerned with the *all* of life. The world is not cut into two mutually exclusive segments: one of secular affairs which religion must disregard; the other composed of religious belief and rituals.

Second, that religion sees all mankind as riding in the same boat, not bobbing about on a lot of separate life rafts bearing the labels of denominations, nations, cultures, or races. We ride out the storms together, or we go down together.

Third, it is not enough for man to profess oneness with other men; he must act it out. More than wearing the garment of religious identification, he must accept its ethical and moral obligations.

The substance of religion is in persons who deeply yearn to know what is good and how it may obtain; it is not merely the claim of personal sacredness, but the binding of oneself to it through respect and sensitivity toward the sacredness of all. It is not enough to boast of the gift of rational intelligence. The substance of religion is to nurture reason—to work it, to apply it, and to defend it.

The Power of the Word

Unitarian Universalists are notably unenthusiastic about proselytizing, but a new zeal for "telling our side of the story" has blossomed among us. Radio and television are increasingly used for presenting our point of view on religious and public issues. I have just completed ten years of regular radio and occasional television appearances, and I can demonstrate by some rather amazing statistics that these powerful media are fertile sources of new Unitarian Universalists. In fact, I am more convinced than ever that there are hundreds of thousands of unchurched religious liberals who are still completely unaware of what Unitarian Universalism represents. Culturally, we are conditioned to think of organized religion in terms of the conventional triumvirate, "Protestant, Catholic, and Jewish." But, in a very real sense, we are the largest and most significant segment of a *fourth* faith—Religious Liberalism!

With the support of the Laymen's League, the organized manpower of our movement, there has been, in recent years, a vigorous educational program through advertisements in selected magazines. Thousands upon thousands of inquiries for further information have been elicited. Any form of personal pressure to join a church is repugnant to us, but response to our educational efforts indicates that it would be shortsighted and selfish for us to withhold information on something about which we are ourselves so enthusiastic, and which strikes such a responsive chord in so many who were previously unaware of our existence. Ours is a live and thrilling option for the many who are dissatisfied with traditional religious institutions, but who do not yet know that another and deeply appealing alternative is available to them. Our new members repeatedly tell us of their intense regret at having gone so many years without discovering the Unitarian Universalist church. "We simply did not know that such a church existed and no one bothered to tell us," they say. We now sense, with fresh appreciation, our obligation to spread as widely as possible a knowledge of our history, our aims, our principles, and the basis of our church life. More than ever before, the time is ripe to resist the religious homogenization of American life by bringing together all who desire to advance the cause of freedom and human fulfillment through liberal religion.

One of our most effective tools for this purpose is the written word. Through the Unitarian Universalist Association, we now support an extremely broad publications program which includes magazines, pamphets, books, and newsletters. Divisions of the program are:

The Pamphlet Commission: a large selection of attractively styled and crisply written pamphlets is available on a variety of subjects of interest to potential members, new members, and established members. These pamphlets are distributed by the hundreds of thousands in our churches and gathering places and are used in various ways by organized groups throughout the denomination.

The Register-Leader: this monthly magazine is the oldest continually published religious journal in America, having been launched in 1821 as *The Christian Register,* and merging in 1961 with the *Universalist Leader.* It is primarily a denominational magazine, but it specializes in articles dealing with subjects of interest to people concerned with liberal religion generally.

The Beacon Press: a major publishing house whose corporate stock is wholly owned by the Unitarian Universalist Association. Its function is to produce books of a serious, general, and often controversial, nature. Beacon hard-cover and paper-back editions are prominently displayed in bookstores throughout our continent, and in many countries overseas. It is the purpose of Beacon Press to make a spirited contribution to the world's cultural, intellectual and religious life through an energetic program of quality publishing which emphasizes the pre-eminence of the human spirit.

It is under the Beacon label that our religious education curricula have been issued, and, interestingly enough, some of our best customers are of other denominations. They like our books on the prophets and heroes of the Old Testament, our story collections for children, and our biographies of famous religious personalities, because these books do their job in a skilled, colorful manner, without special pleading.

In 1947, Beacon Press had a feeble total of seventeen titles on its back list and a few dozen outlets. Now it has hundreds of titles and booksellers in every major city of the world.

Social Outreach

The impact of our denomination is also expressed on the denominational level by the Unitarian Universalist Fellowship for Social Justice. Established in 1908 by a group of ministers and laymen under the leadership of Dr. John Haynes Holmes, the UUFSJ is today doing the most dynamic work in its history. Membership in it is voluntary, and the organization does not pretend to represent all of us. It does unite the energies of the more socially concerned ministers and laymen in our fold, and provides an effective vehicle for direct action on pressing public issues.

Like the Service Committee, the UUFSJ has changed its emphases with changing conditions. In the 1930's it was one of the organized groups which pitted its strength against the incipient native fascism of the Father Coughlins and Huey Longs. In the 1940's its efforts were mobilized to remove the vestiges of racial discrimination from our churches and to strengthen integration movements in our society as a whole.

At the present time, the UUFSJ maintains an office and a small staff in Washington, D. C., where our interests in strengthened civil liberties, in the maintenance of church-state separation, in the United Nations and foreign policy affairs, are fostered. A recent innovation, which has been highly successful, is an annual fall conclave of religious liberals in Washington for intensive study of impending public issues. A newsletter, program aids, and field trips are provided to UUFSJ local chapters all across the continent.

Other action groups in the denomination include the Liberal Religious Peace Fellowship, which represents a merger of the Unitarian Pacifist Fellowship and the Aden Ballou Fellowship (Universalist) and joins the efforts of those ministers and laymen who are vitally concerned with the wel-

fare of Unitarian Universalist conscientious objectors, and
the Unitarian Universalist Society for Alcohol Education,
whose members practice their prerogative, as religious liberals, to band together in behalf of temperance and the prevention and cure of alcoholism.

Of growing importance is the Adult Education section of
the Unitarian Universalist Association. This department
provides expert guidance and materials for the study of religious and social issues in local churches and fellowships, including help in organizing their own social action, human relations, and adult education committees. Of special interest
to many readers of this book may be a collection of tape re-
cordings and a packet for study of the reports of commissions
of a project entitled "The Free Church in a Changing
World."

In all of this we have tried not to forget the still isolated
religious liberal, the individual or family living where there
is as yet no Unitarian Universalist group. For them there is
the Church of the Larger Fellowship, with a headquarters
and minister at 25 Beacon Street, Boston. Weekly printed
sermons, newsletters, and religious education materials are
sent to members who now extend through forty countries.
Albert Schweitzer is perhaps the most renowned member
of the CLF.

On the Move

News from the Unitarian Universalist world has never
been more exciting than it is in this age of revolutionary
change. Major adventures are on the drafting board or actually under way at every level of our movement. We are
constructing a staggering number of new church buildings.
In May of 1963, meeting at Chicago, the Association of Universalist Women and the Unitarian Women's Alliance merged
into one as the Unitarian Universalist Woman's Federation,
and the new combined group is in the midst of a major shift

of emphasis toward "the moral and ethical issues in problems of human relations." The Laymen's League is conducting an experiment in lay communication on those matters which most vitally affect the daily lives and thoughts of religious liberals. The Unitarian Universalist Service Committee is in the midst of a "grand design" for an imaginative expansion of program. In the fall of 1963 the first president of the Unitarian Universalist Association, Dr. Dana McLean Greeley, accompanied by the director of the newest agency of the denomination, the Department of World Churches, the Reverend Max Gaebler, made a trip around the world, visiting countless liberal religious contacts on the globe.

American Unitarian Universalists are in close contact with religious liberals in other parts of the world through the International Association for Religious Freedom, whose headquarters and secretariat are at The Hague in the Netherlands, This small but compact organization held an historic convocation in Chicago in August, 1958, which attracted hundreds of delegates from liberal religious bodies in Europe and Asia, representing Christian, Moslem, Buddhist, Shintoist, and Jewish affiliations.

New ideas, fresh approaches, experimentation, and wise planning and action are combining to give the historic Unitarian Universalist tradition revived and revised relevance to the religious needs and shifting patterns of our time. This must not, and does not, mean that we will grow careless of the profound distinction between being an ecclesiastical or missionary assembly line and being a religious fellowship bent on uniting the efforts of the largest possible number of like-minded people. Our present strength and future promise promote confidence that our era of greatest usefulness and effectiveness is dawning. Dr. Frederick May Eliot wrote: "The only really serious possibility of failure to meet the apparent opportunity now facing Unitarianism lies in the very center of its own spiritual life; and, if the history of the movement may be taken as indicating the probabilities for the future, there is not likely to be failure here. What I have in mind is that recurring infusion of new spiritual sensitiveness and insight which has characterized the movement from the beginning. . . ."

I cannot begin to describe adequately the gratitude I feel for the privilege of being a Unitarian Universalist minister at this particular juncture of history. Less than a generation ago it appeared that both Unitarianism and Universalism were destined to shrivel into ingrown, insignificant sects. Today we have churches and fellowships in every corner of the continent, and our rate of growth is almost enough to make a man believe in miracles. We find ourselves exploring vast, new horizons of service and expansion. To be able to say that I am part of this unfolding destiny, that I am able to make some contribution to its fulfillment, is to express my utter joy at being a member of a unique ministry serving a unique movement. I am a free man in a free religious society, which is actually making freedom prosper at a time when liberty is everywhere under attack.

Dr. Ellsworth Huntington of Yale, who made a study of the names in *Who's Who in America,* wrote: "The productivity of the Unitarians in supplying leaders of the first rank has been 150 times as great as that of the remainder of the population."

I would be less than human if I did not take pride in this astonishing assessment of religious leadership. But my aim, as a Unitarian Universalist minister, is not to compile and publish comparative statistics of our claims to *very important people*. What I care about most is that our faith appeals to, and gives inspiration to, ordinary people with little sparks of courage, who say and do *rather* difficult and different things, who think *somewhat* new thoughts (at least, new to them), and who follow *small* insights in the absence of big ones.

These are the people we want and need, as well as the re-nowned leaders.

I acknowledge with humility and gratitude that we have no exclusive claims to the liberal spirit, nor to social concern and service. Under many labels, people are committed to essentially the same goals and hopes which motivate us. I sincerely hope that in this heady era of growth, we will face with special candor our weaknesses and shortcomings. Some of us slip into a dogmatism no different, psychologically, than that of the proverbial Presbyterian "just off his knees." We are still overwhelmingly a "white" movement, and I must add sadly that there are still a few churches and fellowships in the Deep South where there are bars to Negro members. We are everywhere making progress toward racially integrated con-gregations, but that progress is not nearly so rapid as it should be. People of all racial, national, and religious back-grounds *are cordially welcome* in most of our churches. The gap between things as they are and things as they ought to be is an offense until it is bridged.

NINE

THE COURAGE TO LIVE

Human life is a struggle—against frustration, ignorance, suffering, evil, the maddening inertia of things in general; but it is also a struggle for something, and for something which our experience tells us can be achieved in some measure. . . .

JULIAN HUXLEY, *Evolution in Action*

HAVELOCK ELLIS once said that the more a man tries to say precisely what is in his own heart, the more he finds that he is speaking for millions of strangers the world over. The deeper we get down to our own fundamentals, the more deeply we represent those of other people. As I near the end of this experiment in writing out the reasons why I am what I am, the more necessary it becomes to tell what Unitarian Universalism contributes to my courage to live. I have spoken in considerable detail of our motives of service and self-renunciation, but these motives can be followed only by those who first have a self to renounce. I am a religious liberal because the religious movement of which I am a part not only permits but encourages me to say what is deepest in my self and in my thoughts about life.

Like all other humans, I live on borrowed time. I never know when my string of time will run out. I have no way of anticipating what tragedies may befall me at the next step, the next ring of the telephone, the next rising of the sun. My notion of religious fulfillment is to learn how to accept this fate with a ringing affirmation of all that makes life worth living. Religion is my inspiration to be a creative, cooperative human being in spite of the fact that life may crush me at any moment and death blot me out. As a skeptic, I cannot comfort myself with supernatural promises. I know that human existence contains its irreducible elements of tragedy and incompleteness. I know that I cannot really comprehend the totality of things. I am finite. For me, the fundamental question of life is not "why" but "how." How shall I live while I live? This is the core question. In answering, it matters very much what I believe. As we read in the Apocryphal book called *Ecclesiasticus:*

> Accept no person against thine own soul,
> And let no reverence for any man cause thee to fall.
> But let the counsel of thine own heart stand:
> For there is none more faithful unto thee than it.
> For a man's mind is sometimes wont to bring him tidings,
> More than seven watchmen, that sit above in a high tower.

What do I believe about the compensations for tragedy? I believe that almost every tragic occurrence *has* its compensation. A person deprived of sight may develop astonishing sensitivity of ear. So also are there mental compensations, bridges which we build toward sanity, again and again, even when we feel that our nerve fibers have taken all they can take.

Thanksgiving Day is sometimes a perverse reminder of the many reasons we have for feeling unthankful. There are few who do not know the pain of rejection, the anguish of confidences betrayed, the confusion of fretting over approval and disapproval, the ache of loneliness. Life has a way of turning us into caricatures of ourselves. In the 25th Psalm we read: "Turn thou to me, and be gracious to me; for I am lonely and afflicted." We cannot know the character of the psalmist's loneliness, but we do know the character of our own. We need not be caricatures. Loneliness is real. For man, being alive means being in a body; a body separate from all other bodies. And being separate means being alone. The uniqueness and awesomeness of man is that he *knows* he is alone. Aloneness has its compensations.

From Sausalito, California, came the fascinating story of how one of Hollywood's swashbuckling film characters, Sterling Hayden, fell into what the writer of Hebrews calls "the hands of the living God." Hayden disobeyed a court order and sailed his children to Tahiti in a broken-down schooner. He left behind him a letter which is a deeply revealing human document. "I have an idea and an understanding of what is within me," he wrote. "I may well be wrong in my outlook, and it doesn't really matter too much. What I think does matter is that a man has an obligation to live up to what he believes. . . ."

For years, he went on, he had been selling himself out: "Just recall the pathetic trash I have made, month after month, year after year . . . you can't do this. I am a decent enough man; not too bright perhaps, but impelled by some ideas as to conviction and principle. I was sustained by my inner determination to break out . . . and now is the time to go."

I found myself strangely moved by Mr. Hayden's confrontation of himself. He could never achieve in a movie such an honest portrayal of a man willing to take upon himself the loneliness of conviction. Before he went aboard his ship, *Wanderer,* and raised her sails, he must have been somewhere alone. And so are we. Convictions arise out of our aloneness, and they are its compensation, if we have the courage to accept the destiny of loneliness which is every man's.

Is it really so that each of us is alone? Is not our aloneness largely dissolved in the intimacies of love and friendship: Do not an ideally married couple overcome separateness? "Love consists in this," wrote Rainer Rilke, "that two solitudes protect, and touch, and greet one another." But man and

woman remain alone even in the most affectionate union. We
do not penetrate into one another's innermost center of being, no matter how strong our love, because it is our human
greatness to have an unassailable inner core which is ours
alone. My religion recognizes and respects that impenetrable
center of my being. It gives me leave to find my convictions
within it, and to develop within solitude of soul my sense of
compensation. This is another way of saying that the world
is undoubtedly a terrible place, but I love it. I am alone in
the world because I am a man, but being alone I can look
out upon the world and love it, and cooperate with others,
who are also alone, to transform it. This, I say, is where faith
enters and makes its presence felt. As long as I have the
courage to accept my aloneness and my vulnerability to
tragedy, as long as I am brave enough to know that, even in
my own warm home I am but on a visit, as long as I can
face the fact that everything I build will someday crumble,
I am free to give that which endures on this earth: the spirit
in which I understand and meet life's tremendous strains.
This I pass on to my wife, my children, my friends, my parishioners, my associates. I live so that Man may live. Any
faith smaller than this will not console me in my transitory
defeats, nor comfort me in my moments of despair, nor give
me the courage to push through.

Cassius says to Brutus:

> There is a tide in the affairs of men,
> Which, taken at the flood, leads on to fortune;
> Omitted, all the voyage of their life
> Is bound in shallows and in miseries.

I do not believe that there is any *one* moment which
"taken at the flood" leads us to the fulfilling courage to stand
and be ourselves. All we are and believe, all we do and work
for and love, is *constantly* under the pressure of disappointment. Yet, the tides keep rising. We salvage. We compensate.

We cultivate the strength that comes with sharing, with caring, with reaching out, with bestowing where we can, the meanings we discover in the core of our aloneness. This is the truth of Whitehead's famous definition: "Religion is what a man does with his solitariness." There is reverence in my religion for my solitariness. There is no compulsion in liberal religion to intrude upon my aloneness with public revelations and salvation systems. My solitariness is honored. There is respect for *my* human condition, and for the way in which I choose to enter into communion with others. There is recognition that the real religious decision is *what I decide to do, together with others,* and that the role of the church is not to bend my will but to give strength and flexibility to my willing. The will is in the self. Out of the self comes the character of the deeds which make for individuality.

In our intermediate fate, there is no substantial variety, because we are all subject to anxiety, accident, and disappointment. In our ultimate fate, there is no variety whatsoever, because we all must die. But it matters greatly how we deal with our anxieties, accidents and disappointments. It matters greatly what we believe in while we are around. It matters to *us,* even if it may not to the universe, what purposes we set for the days of our years. I am a Unitarian Universalist because I do not require or want revelatory proof of purpose. I have faith in purpose in the midst of the unknown, because I know that the purposes I choose in my aloneness are themselves the sources of my courage, my balance, and my compensation.

To live is to grow, and to grow means to change enough to be able to play a creative part in change itself. I am acquainted with a play-therapy clinic for children, where the first reactions of one child who was brought for treatment was to raise his arm in protection or attack whenever an adult approached. One of the teachers worked and worked with this child until that exquisite moment came when an accept-

ing smile finally broke through on the boy's face, and he
dropped his arm, his symbol of fear.

The history books will never celebrate this teacher as one
of the earth's liberators. Her name will never be joined with
those of Socrates, Jefferson, and Darwin, but, in essence, she
is a liberator of the most precious quality there is: human
courage. In this she deserves to rank with the greatest, because
she shares the emancipating intentions of those who are
greatest. And so may we all.

I cannot *prove* the purposes through which we find the
courage to take our stand on the side of growth. I do believe
in these purposes, and not just naively. I believe in them
because I am so sure of the liberating possibilities in men and
women. The comfort of my religion rests not on any of the
conventional but questionable proofs of God's personal concern and care. It rests squarely on the encouragement I have
found in my aloneness, and in an appreciation of the aloneness of others, to accept and trust life without such proofs.
If the world of nature is impersonal, so be it. If the universe
plays no favorites—or, as Einstein put it, "God does not play
dice"—isn't that after all a necessary condition of whatever
dependability we can find? My liberal religion offers me the
comfort of spiritual solitude in a world where I can hope-
fully rise to meet, or compensate for, most of my problems;
where, in fact, I can intelligently anticipate many of the
stresses I must solve or bear. In brief, mine is a religion
which cares more about me *as a person*—my potential resources and strengths—than it does about theological explanations or atonements of the dilemmas and failures which
beset me. My courage to live is not mediated by priests or
revelations. It is cultivated in the recesses of my essential
aloneness, and challenged by the opportunities of communion with others. I know that my ultimate fate is not in my
hands, but the human version of fate is. The element of
tragedy I cannot always control, but beyond tragedy I may

choose the purposes by which my life may be guided. My human limitations I cannot abolish, but within the limitations are the meanings I am free to create.

I count it as one of the great and good fortunes of our generation that a superb poet, yearning for a metaphor of the twentieth century's spiritual dilemmas, turned to the Book of Job. In writing *J. B.*, Archibald MacLeish ran a dangerous gauntlet of literary risk. The Book of Job is probably the greatest work of Hebrew literature which has come down to us. It is no small problem to do justice in a modern work to its insight, its imagery, its richness of symbolism, and its depth of feeling. MacLeish has given us a worthy Job of our time, and he tests his fidelity in terms of our calamities and explanations. In a highly imaginative setting, MacLeish successfully avoids sanctimoniousness and religious sentimentality without losing any of the intimacy of the grandeur of J. B.'s terrible trial. I love the way he has Zuss and Nickles play God and Satan by putting on a pair of appropriate masks. It is wonderful to have them speaking through their masks with heavenly detachment, and then removing their masks to make very human and salty comments about supernatural affairs. The masks produce what is for me one of the most moving perceptions of the entire drama. Nickles after donning his mask for the first time, tears it off in a kind of cold sweat. "Those eyes *see*," he says:

> They see the *world*. They do. They see it.
> From going to and fro in the earth.
> From walking up and down, they see it.
> I know what Hell is now—to *see*.
> Consciousness of consciousness. . . .*

Has anyone ever experienced a moment of searing, conscious insight without knowing what Nickles meant when

* Houghton Mifflin Co.

he ripped off his mask? To know life is to *see*—to be gripped by the terrible pain and wonder of it.

As a poet, Mr. MacLeish is very much of this world. His J. B. is also very much of this world. J. B. is a happy, prosperous businessman, surrounded by a family of all-American children and loved by an intelligent, attractive wife. He thinks well of his fellow men and is sincerely grateful to God for his abundance and good fortune. Then God begins to enlighten him about the true nature of life. The afflictions stab with senseless abandon and brutality. One by one his children are murderously destroyed. To cap all this, his business is blown up, leaving him penniless and suffering from hideous radiation burns. In a final blow, his wife deserts him in disgust for his failure to defend himself.

At this point, MacLeish introduces typical soothsayers of our generation—a conventional preacher, a psychoanalyst, and a Marxist—who attempt to explain J. B.'s catastrophes and to console him with their characteristic panaceas. His first comforter, the Marxist, tells J. B. that he is being punished by historical necessity:

> God is History. If you offend Him
> Will not History dispense with you?
> History has no time for innocence.

The second comforter, the psychoanalyst, informs J. B. that he is punishing himself unnecessarily in the depths of his unconscious, mindless guilt.

The third, a ponderous, pastoral type, insists that J. B. is being punished for the unpardonable sin of having been born:

> . . . Guilt is reality!
> The one reality there is!
> All mankind are guilty always!

J. B., in his misery, rejects all three. "What is my fault?" he cries. "What have I done?" The clergyman thunders back:

> What is your fault? Man's heart is evil!
> What have you done? Man's will is evil.
> Your fault, your sin, are heart and will:
> .... Your sin is
> Simple. You were born a man!

J. B. crouches lower in his rags and agony, and speaks very softly:

> Yours is the cruelest comfort of them all,
> Making the Creator of the Universe
> The miscreator of mankind—
> A party to the crimes He punishes...

At this point MacLeish makes the same abrupt switch we find in the ancient Book of Job. God relents and rewards J. B. for his unwavering loyalty. He restores to J. B. his affluence, his health, and his wife. To say that this resolution cheats is to put it mildly.

What really matters in J. B., as it does in Job, is not that a happy ending is awkwardly patched on, but that there is an epilogue of interpretations and affirmations which go to the heart of the human dilemma. There are first of all the unforgettable words placed in God's mouth by the ancient author of Job and retained virtually intact by MacLeish:

> Where wast thou when I laid the foundations of the earth...
> Hast thou commanded the morning
> Can'st thou bind the sweet influence of the Pleiades?

Who is man to feel that he must have an explanation for everything that happens? Who is man to believe that his pain and pleasure can only be understoood as reward and punishment; as the willful giving or withholding of his God? Is it man who gives the horse strength or makes the eagle

mount? Reward and punishment are not God's themes but
man's own. The universe does not reward or punish; it
simply *is*. God does not reward or punish. God *is*.

And to this J. B. and his wife respond, as we, if we have
such wisdom, will also respond. Into any life may come
events too terrible to understand, but not because they are
willed by a malignant universe. The universe is neither just
nor unjust; the universe does not curse or bless. Man's answer is not to seek justice in the heavens, but to seek it in
himself. "You wanted justice, and there was none," J. B.'s
wife says. But she offers her love.

The universe gives life—the precious gift of life—and man's
answer is love: love of God, love of the universe, for making
life possible; and love of those who share the gift. This kind
of love is wholly man's to give or withhold.

In this violent century, J. B. and J. B.'s wife are abstracts
of each and every one of us. As such they are written larger
than life-size, so that their plight overwhelms us not only
with pity and terror, but with reverence for the human race
of which we are a part. We are human and we are mortal.
We did not create the universe, and we need not despair
that we cannot explain all its mysteries, conflicts, and personal catastrophes. We know that suffering comes, that it can
come to us, and that when it does we must bear it. We know
also that it comes to others, and that when it does, our task is
not to justify or explain but to ease and comfort. We are
born into a world of many evils, some of them made by man,
and some of them made by more than man. Our task is not
so much to know from whence these evils come as how they
may be resisted, or borne, or overcome.

We speak of justice, but the lesson of Job and *J. B.* is that
the only justice we will find is that which we make among
men. We speak of love, but the lesson of Job and *J. B.* is that
the only love we will know is that which we exchange with
one another. The Book of Job was written to destroy the

THE COURAGE TO LIVE

monstrous doctrine that God willfully and personally rewards and punishes. *J. B.* was written to remind us that if we
look to heaven for an explanation of our generation's travails
and terrors we will find only emptiness and despair. The universe creates but does not legislate. The universe gives life
but does not judge. Justice is a human genius, not a divine
one. It may err and be corrected. Misfortune is a human experience, not a cosmic punishment. If all things are to come
out right in the end we do not know it. What we do know
is that there is no substitute for blowing "on the coals of the
human heart."

The answer to what we call the injustices of life is love—
our "love of life in spite of life." The universe gives life, and
man gives life a soul, but only if he loves in the midst of his
thralldom, in spite of suffering, injustice, and death. From
Job to *J. B.* the lesson is this: we are *not* called upon to justify the ways of God to man; we are *always* called upon to
justify the ways of man to man.

In Job and *J. B.* I find stirring parables of what my religion
means to my courage to live. I do not love life because
"God will take care of me." My reason tells me that the
universe is not organized to look after my personal welfare.
The universe has given me life. By placing that life in a body
separate from all other bodies, the universe has also granted
me an unassailable core of inner being which is mine and
mine alone to cultivate and deepen. No priest or revelation
can mediate between my solitariness and Life-as-a-Whole. I
love life because, although it leaves me in an ultimate sense
alone, it brings me into communion with everyone else's
aloneness. In solitariness I sense how intimately I am tied
to all from whom I am separated. My religion is the finding
of self and others. It is not only my courage to live with
myself, in all my stark individuality and aloneness, but it
also is my basic source of the power to live serviceably with
others.

Immortality for Skeptics

In his absorbing book, *The Nature of the Universe,** astronomer Fred Hoyle writes: "Here we are in this wholly fantastic Universe with scarcely a clue as to whether our existence has any real significance. No wonder then that many people feel the need for some belief that gives them a sense of security, and no wonder that they become very angry with people like me who say that this security is illusory." Most Unitarian Universalists would agree with Mr. Hoyle that there is nothing to be gained in this life by theological self-deception, at least, not for them. Yet, when we come to certain specific kinds of beliefs, which are supposed to impart a sense of security, the issues are something less than simple. Take, for example, the belief which is so ardently cultivated and celebrated during the great Christian festival of Easter: the belief in personal immortality. Justice is not done to this belief simply by declaring it to be self-delusion. We must understand that this belief, for many people, is an effective means of combating the lonely prospect of dying, and making life more tolerable. We do live, as Mr. Hoyle says, in a fantastic universe, and with each advance in science it seems to grow even more fantastic. Those who find sustaining hope in the Christian message of immortality are struggling in their own way with a universal problem. We may disagree with them, as I do, but we have no right to level a charge of self-deception against any open and sincere effort to find courage and purpose at the heart of life. I have dealt too long and too intimately with people facing death to feel anything but compassion and sympathy for the various means by which fortitude and acceptance are mobilized.

I sat, not so long ago, at the bedside of a man who knew that within a few weeks lung cancer would snuff out his life. I asked him how he felt about what lay ahead. He told me

* Harper & Brothers, p. 139.

that he was able to feel quite serene about death. He felt, with Socrates, that death cannot be a harsh or evil thing. He went on: "I would be less than honest, however, if I did not tell you that I have qualms about *dying*." A distinction between death and dying! And how valid a distinction it is. Death is unknown, but it is the universal end of all living things. Death is nothingness or another life, and surely neither holds terror. We remain *alone* in our anticipations of dying. No communication with others can remove this aloneness. Those who love us can touch and protect, but they cannot share or hide the fact that it is our dying and ours alone which awaits ahead. Can we stand this loneliness? The world's many theologies and immortality myths bear witness to man's doubt that he can stand it without the comfort of metaphysical certainties.

Yet, there are those who find small solace in the promises of resurrection and eternal life. Most religious liberals are among this group, and the number constantly grows. A recent survey of beliefs among Methodist laymen discloses that a surprisingly large minority harbors doubts about the resurrection and its traditional meaning. I myself am unimpressed by the Christian gospel of Easter. It seems to me to be a quite impossible and fantastic doctrine. My ministry is basically to people whose thoughts and experiences lead them to doubt the adequacy of the traditional Christian message of personal immortality, and to seek for something more nearly suited to their emotional and reasoned needs. There is nothing strange or perverse in this point of view. It grows on a person with reflection. It may flicker first as a reaction against the Christian gospel. If Jesus was, as orthodox Christians claim, a divine being, his rising from the dead says nothing about a mere man's ability to conquer death. Men are not deities; they are human beings. To celebrate the resurrection of a deity tells us nothing about the prospects for human beings. In good logic, only those who *disbelieve* in the deity of Jesus should be able to derive any real comfort from accepting the story of his resurrection. It seems to have no proper place in a contemporary, rational view of life. That early Christians believed in a resurrection is no sound reason, in itself, for believing it today. Everybody believed in supernatural happenings and wonders two thousand years ago. They believed, for example, that mental illness was caused by the presence of tiny devils inside a person's body. We happen to know better today. It can be said with much the same assurance that we happen also to know better about resurrections. Moreover, our study of history makes it clear that Jesus did not bring the hope of personal afterlife into the world, because not only the hope but the belief in it were the possession of peoples long before his time.

Some metaphysicians tell us that even if we discard all questions of Jesus' role, there are still convincing psychical and spiritual proofs of personal immortality. But after examining these "proofs," it is quite possible for an honest mind to conclude that they are inadequate. There are also metaphysical proofs for the existence of angels, but the angels do not necessarily exist.

There are impressive forms of poetically expressed belief in personal survival after death. They come from persons, such as Wordsworth, who base their faith on what they call the intimations and intuitions of inner experience. Men of high intelligence in the ancient world—thoughtful, sensitive men like Cicero of Rome and Plato of Greece—found a faith in personal immortality in their conviction that human life at its best is too precious to end with death, and that survival is required for the fulfillment of ideal desires. Emerson had similar feelings, and wrote:

> What is excellent,
> As God lives, is permanent;
> Hearts are dust, hearts' loves remain;
> Heart's love will meet thee again.

Yet, even under the spell of beautiful thoughts so beautifully articulated, there are some of us who are not persuaded by our sense of human worth to require a personal continuance after death of those who enhance that worth in life. In other words, traditional concepts of immortality do not become more valid simply because they are associated with a morally satisfying view of human life. Feeling, of itself, no matter how elevated, does not signify personal survival. Compassionate human behavior is not inspiring because it whispers to us of some concrete plan of immortality; it is inspiring in itself and on its own merits. The teachings of Jesus are not guides to ethical growth because they are linked with beliefs about his resurrection. They are guides because their worth is implicit in human conduct.

Why I exist, nobody on earth is capable of telling me; but, since I do exist, let me strive to give my existence a brightness and glory by setting up for myself the loftiest goals I can reasonably hope to achieve. This is my religious view. Is there a kind of immortality which fits and augments such a view? To me there is, and I am joined in it by many of my fellow Unitarian Universalists. Interestingly enough, there is nothing new about this view. Since long before the time of Jesus it has been cultivated by some of the Chinese religions. It has been known and cherished by Buddhists for nearly twenty-five hundred years. It is belief in the *immortality of character, of conduct and thought, of influence.* In no way does this take from me the loneliness of dying. I know that dying is something I must face alone and with honest apprehension. But I have something to live and die for: not a personal survival in which I cannot believe, but a present and lasting immortality of influence in which I can believe.

Whatever such an observation may be worth, this is a truly democratic idea of immortality. It is an affirmation that everyone is immortal since whatever men do lives on "somewhere, somehow, somewhen." The evil men do is as immor-

tal as the good. There is an immortality of the ignoble as well
as the noble, of the brutish as well as the sublime, of selfishness as well as generosity, of stupidity as well as wisdom.
Immortality is complete. It encompasses the whole of what
one is.

When we reason together about the truths and mysteries
of life, there is one all-powerful reality: the humanity of
which we are individual expressions is a product of the sense
and nonsense of our fathers. We are the living immortality of
those who came before us. In like manner, those who come
after us will be the harvest of the wisdom and folly we ourselves are sowing. To let this reality permeate and drench
the consciousness is to introduce ourselves to a grand conception of immortality which makes yearnings for some form
of personal afterlife seem meager indeed. So long as there
is an ongoing stream of humanity I have life. This is my immortality. I am a renewed and renewing link in the chain
of humanity. My memory and particularity are personal,
transitory, finite; my substance is boundless and infinite. The
immortality in which I believe affirms my unity with human-
kind. My unity with mankind gives meaning to my desire
to practice reverence for life. It is pride in being, and pride
in belonging to all being. I do not welcome the fact that
dying waits ahead for me. Yet, I know that I must die, and
I will attempt to do so with reasonable fortitude and honor.
Death, on the other hand, presents me with no special problems. It cannot be an evil condition. Of immortality, my
mind and heart can cherish only the kind I have described.
My religion affirms rather than denies the freedom in which
I have discussed these matters. As a Unitarian Universalist
I grant that there *may* be a personal existence after death.
No one, in advance, can really tell. But there is one certain
immortality, the realism of which we *can* know in advance.
It connects us with every human being who shares this earth
with us. It joins us in unbroken line with all who have

mortally passed from this earth before us. It unites us with all who are yet unborn. By the glow of this idea of immortality, I read with renewed appreciation John Donne's words:

"No man is an Island, entire of itself; every man is a piece of the Continent, a part of the main; if a Clod be washed away by the Sea, Europe is the less, as well as if a Promontory were; as well as if a Manor of thy friends or of thine own were; any man's death diminishes me, because I am involved in Mankind; and therefore never send to know for whom the bell tolls; it tolls for thee."

For those of us who can live no longer under the spell of traditional beliefs in resurrections and personal afterlives, the larger message of immortality need not be lost. Fundamentally, it is a message of renewed and ongoing life, and of the wonder that his thoughts and deeds are every man's real immortality.

If Jesus Is the Answer

I once heard a radio commercial, in which the announcer, on behalf of a religious publishing house, was promoting the sale of a book entitled *Dr. Luke, Beloved Physician*. "Read this *factual* account of how most modern medical techniques were anticipated by the author of the Third Gospel," said the voice. This would be amusing if it did not represent such blatant cynicism about the credulousness and ignorance of potential buyers. There are no sources of information about Luke's medical techniques. Offering a "factual account" of something for which there are no existing facts is a neat trick, but it is not religion. The same kind of problem confronts us when we attempt to deal with Jesus. "Factual accounts" are plentiful, but facts are exceedingly scarce.

On a trip to Milwaukee I saw several huge public billboards bearing a message, "Christ Is The Answer." If Christ is the answer, what are the questions? An answer, unless it is preceded by meaningful questions, is not much of an answer at all. Steve Allen, whose comedy is often a commentary on current human foibles, has used a routine which he calls "The Question Man." Satirizing the vacuity of quiz programs, he poses as a seedy professorial type, who supplies the questions for people's answers. Behind the satire is a basic truth. It is frequently easier to supply answers than it is to ask the right questions. Unitarian Universalism is an "asking" religion, and unashamedly so. As one of its adherents I feel no qualms about asking what should be a very obvious question: How do we know who Jesus is or was?

The answer must be discovered in the writings about him, and these are the Gospels. Nothing is known of Jesus except what is to be found in them. All other literature of his time and place is lacking in a single, dependable reference. The letters of Paul have much to say *about* Jesus, but Paul confesses that he never knew Jesus in the flesh. What Paul wrote was "interpretation." If this is true of Paul, it is even more true of at least one of the Gospels, John. If Paul was far removed from the personality of Jesus, then John, according to most scholars, was even farther removed. So, what we have left to answer our question must be found in Matthew, Mark, and Luke. We know nothing about these three books from any other source, and we know little if anything about their authors. Scholars generally agree that the names, Matthew, Mark, and Luke, have meager historical credibility. Whatever validity these Gospels have to offer must be confirmed within the context of the books themselves. When we turn to an examination of the Gospel material, we find that in large part the three are identical, so that the whole of the available material about Jesus is about one-third what it seems to be. Most scholars believe that Matthew and Luke copied from Mark. This suggests that Matthew and Luke had no first-hand knowledge of Jesus, since what is not copied sounds even less like authentic, personal observation. But what about Mark? Did he know Jesus? If he did, the acquaintanceship was not overly intimate. There is not a single reference in Mark to the appearance of Jesus, something that seems unlikely if the author had experienced contact with such an apparently vivid personality. We are forced to the conclusion that the author of Mark's Gospel could have known people who *did* know Jesus, and he may even have been a younger contemporary. Matthew and Luke wrote at least a generation later, and John more nearly a century later.

Having taken this quick tour through the scholarly realm of New Testament study, we find certain questions to be inescapable. How can a person be the answer about whom there is no first-hand knowledge, and very sparse second- or third-hand information? Historical knowledge, in and of itself, may not be the only means of judging, but what other justifications are there for the claim that Jesus is the answer?

Intelligent, sensitive, dedicated people, who are fully aware of the historical implications of Biblical scholarship, still say that Jesus is the answer, as they did when the World Council of Churches met in Evanston a few summers ago. We, who are puzzled by this, owe it to ourselves to try to understand their position. One fruitful approach is to acquaint ourselves with the viewpoint known popularly as Neo-orthodoxy. Modern Christian theologians such as Reinhold Neibuhr and Paul Tillich lean heavily on a Danish genius of a century ago, Soren Kierkegaard, who probed the mysteries of life through the existentialist technique of looking deeply within himself. By doing this, Kierkegaard convinced himself that he was a chaos of untruth, sinfulness, and alienation from God. If man is created in the image of God, how can this be? Kierkegaard insisted that God is not within man. Saving grace must come from outside. The deeper a man probes into himself, the further he is from ultimate truth.

By looking to his own resources, man has widened the gulf between himself and God. Sin has conquered his precious

free will. The more the individual strives to pull himself up
by his bootstraps and touch the reality of God, the more
he sinks into a state of despair. Even a knowledge of God's
love overwhelms him and makes him more hopelessly conscious of sin. The only answer is for God to take the initia-
tive. God can do this in two ways. One alternative is to lift
man up to the level of God; the other is for God to debase
himself and become a man. Kierkegaard argued that the first
course is unthinkable. He did not adequately explain why it
is unthinkable, but he dismissed the possibility. The second
choice is the only defensible one. God, said Kierkegaard,
came over to man by *becoming* man in the form of Jesus
Christ.

This startling act is not without its drawbacks, according
to Kierkegaard. The human mind is affronted, and the affront
cuts in two directions. Jesus' claim to be God is odiously
offensive to human reason. Any such claim is insulting. At
the same time, it is an attack on human reason to expect
belief that God would dream of becoming a man. The human mind rebels at the absurdity of God becoming a car-
penter whose fate is to hang on a cross as a common criminal
in the insignificant land of Palestine.

With genuine savor, Kierkegaard shaped the paradox and
declared that only the love of God makes it possible for the
mind to accept such an irrational truth. But if you would
be a Christian, Kierkegaard concluded, you must crush reason and take a leap of faith. Thus, becoming a Christian is
an agonizing experience, which bears no resemblance to what
Kierkegaard called the "perpetual Sunday twaddle about
Christianity's . . . sweet consolation." Kierkegaard's Christianity consists of no reasonable summons to live the life of a
good citizen. It is an uncompromising repudiation of reason
in favor of faith. This is what makes Jesus the answer, and
not whether scholarly examination of the Bible delineates
and confirms his mission. It is all right for a Christian to be

intellectually interested in rational studies of religion, but
salvation is another matter. Without the leap of faith, there
is no salvation. Jesus is the answer, not in reason, but in faith.

Kierkegaard sharpens the issue magnificently. He makes
the next question inescapable. Am I prepared to leave reason
behind and go soaring off into what he calls faith? The
answer, obviously, is a resounding *no*. I have no argument
with the notion that Kierkegaard was an authentic Christian
genius, but he has failed to persuade me to abandon my
mind. I *do* have a mind. It may not be an overly impressive
one, but such as it is, it is mine. However I may have come
to possess it—whether from God, or from genes and chromo-
somes, or from education, or from a combination of all three
—I am determined to make the best of it *in my religious
life*. If rational intelligence is part of our given endowment,
it is logically given to be exercised rather than exorcised. If
Jesus can be justified as the answer only on the basis of a
claim that God wishes me to cast out my reasoning abilities,
he cannot be an answer for me.

Fair enough, some of my orthodox friends might say. You
cannot accept on faith that Jesus is the answer. What about
his unsurpassed moral teachings? Can't your reason accept
these as an authentic revelation of God's will?

Historically, Unitarian Universalists have professed a profound reverence for the teachings of Jesus. In fact, an idealized interpretation of Jesus as human teacher and prophet
has characterized our development, and still does. Many of
us consider themselves to be true Christians, not in a Kierke-
gaardian sense, but in terms of the reverence in which they
hold and desire to emulate the teachings of Jesus. If our religion means anything, it means the right to choose this kind
of identity in the religious life. But, are there no disturbing
difficulties in the teachings of Jesus? If the teachings of Jesus
are the answer, which teachings and which Jesus are meant?

An attentive reading of the Gospels can be an unnerving

experience. When Jesus called for turning the other cheek, he offered no prudent exceptions. There are many situations in which turning the other cheek is not only moral but highly practical conduct. On other occasions it might be a way of risking not only one's own safety but that of others as well. If I spotted a man about to detonate an explosive in a crowded Boston subway station, I would be inclined to try to stop him forcibly. Turning the other cheek has something less than universal application in international affairs. The world's leaders do not all agree on a code of ethics, and a foreign policy consisting entirely of turning the other cheek might conceivably lead to the slaughter of a great many innocent people.

It can be argued that Jesus believed in the ultimate conquest of good over evil and based his teaching on such a belief. I happen to believe that there is nothing inevitable about the supremacy of good. In fact, the only goodness I have ever seen count is that which is doggedly and intelligently implemented. What I am saying is simply that I am against turning the other cheek when it is unintelligent and unreasonable to do so. On the other hand, I recognize how plausible and effective turning the other cheek can be in a large percentage of the stresses which afflict ordinary human relations. I attempt, therefore, to practice it, subject to the guidance of reason, and I honor Jesus for the advocacy of it. Then I remember that in another portion of the Gospels Jesus used excessively violent language against the Pharisees and Sadducees. Nothing of cheek-turning there. Which was the real Jesus? Was he both, or neither? "Do not think that I have come to bring peace on earth; I have not come to bring peace, but a sword. For I have come to set a man against his father, and a daughter against her mother, and a daughter-in-law against her mother-in-law; and a man's foes will be those of his own household." Matthew 10:34-36. This is Jesus speaking, according to the writer of Matthew's Gospel. Can it

be the same Jesus who in the same Gospel is reported as saying "Love your enemies . . ."?

The only logical inference is that the true follower of
Jesus will stir up hostilities even within his own family, but
proceed to love the enemies he has made. In truth, there is
no logic in a juxtaposition of these two teachings except the
logic of any man's human inconsistencies. But, if these are
two sides of Jesus' personality, which am I to accept as *the
answer?*

Actually, what religious liberals generally have in mind
when they speak of their reverence for the moral leadership
of Jesus are his most apt and penetrating parables, plus the
precepts of the Sermon on the Mount. With some reserva-
tions about their lack of prudent qualifications, I can warmly
endorse the notion that these are moving and inspiring ethical teachings. I cannot, however, close my mind to other
teachings attributed to Jesus, which strike me as being anything but applicable to today's needs. Should we heed Jesus'
teaching that it is better not to marry? Should we expect, as
he apparently did, the immediate, eschatological termination
of the world, and drop everything to prepare for it?

The point I am trying to make, and it seems to me to be
a very important one, is that the Jesus portrayed in the
Gospels is a confusing and bewildering figure. To refine his
teachings for the modern mind is, as Albert Schweitzer has
so amply demonstrated, a baffling problem. What we really
seem to mean when we say that the "spirit of Jesus" is the
answer to many of our problems is that we would like to try
to the best of our ability to live by the moral goals Jesus
seemed to represent, namely compassion, unselfishness, self-
sacrifice, and goodwill. No one should be upset if, while
agreeing wholeheartedly with this, I suggest that these admirable goals represented by the idealization of Jesus can be
duplicated in all of the world's great religions. It is pertinent
to honor Buddha, Zoroaster, Isaiah, and Confucius, no less

than Jesus, for symbolizing compassion, unselfishness, self-sacrifice, and goodwill.

Jesus is, and will remain, a stirring idealization of what religious liberals hold dear in the religious life. By the same token, religious liberals should be as anxious to avoid fuzzy thinking about Jesus as about other religious symbols. Fortunately the book is far from closed on questions and answers about Jesus. The Dead Sea Scroll material brings fresh excitement to the subject, and I am convinced that there will be many more finds of similarly provocative material.

To me, the important thing about Jesus is not that he was *just* human, but that the human race is capable of producing him. And not him alone, but others like him. And not only in ancient times, but now.

Respectable Praying

Prayer is both a problem and a challenge to the religious liberal. I am almost ashamed for my parents to admit it, but the first and only prayer taught to me as a small child was the familiar "Now I lay me down to sleep. . . ." I am reasonably certain that it did me no great harm, but it took me a good many years to conquer negative feelings toward prayer, and to find a constructive place for it in my religious life. I still experience waves of revulsion at the content of certain types of public prayer, but I can hear something like this by Robert Louis Stevenson with joy and inspiration: "The day returns and brings us the petty round of irritating concerns and duties. Help us to play the man, help us to perform them with laughter and kind faces; let cheerfulness abound with industry. Give us to go blithely on our business all this day, bring us to our resting beds weary and content and undishonored, and grant us in the end the gift of sleep."

This, I would say, is an eminently respectable prayer which any honest man could repeat without feeling craven. Like

John Tyndall, I think "solemnly of the feeling which prompts prayer. It is a power which I should like to see guided, not extinguished—devoted to practicable objects instead of wasted upon air." Prayer *should* trouble the conscientious religious liberal. In many of its customary forms, it is primitive, naive, and frequently selfish. Who can attribute nobility to attempts to cajole and wheedle God into giving us what we personally want, or into veering the order of nature and history for our personal benefit? Huckleberry Finn was a classic practitioner of the kind of prayer that backfires. His Aunt Polly gave him a fish-pole. She also told him that if he prayed hard enough, God would send him whatever he wanted. Huck took this seriously and literally. Several nights in a row he went into the closet of his room and prayed for some fishhooks. He did not receive them. Obviously, there was something wrong with the whole idea of prayer, so Huck gave it up.

This is a familiar problem. It illustrates the importance of the assumptions we make about prayer. If prayer is conceived as a method of getting what we want, as a kind of cosmic lever for prying personally desired answers out of the universe, then, like Huck, we are doomed to futility and frustration. Like him, we will end by renouncing prayer as a snare and a delusion, and we would be quite right about this particular kind of praying.

But suppose we start from an entirely different assumption. Suppose we think of prayer not as a means of commandeering God's attention to our personal wants, but as an approach to the deepest truths about ourselves. Suppose we think of it as a way of shedding new light on our relations with others. Suppose we think of it as an essential religious striving to express truth and tap our resources of love. What then? Do not great vistas of respectable possibilities open before us?

There are many means for getting what we think we want in this world. Money is one. Prestige is another. And personal privilege. There are the various kinds of "pull" we can exert. For children, sometimes a tantrum will produce the most favorable results. In the grown-up world, political leverage will sometimes accomplish wonders. Prayer is not like these. Rather, it is an effort to *become* what we would like to be, and need to be, and ought to be. Proper prayer is not a petition to escape realities. It is an effort to face and understand realities. It is an expression of the desire to grow in spiritual stature, in courage, in strength, and in faith. The purpose of prayer is to transform the person praying, to lift him out of fear and selfishness into serenity, patience, determination. If we can begin to approach prayer in this manner, it assumes an entirely new significance. In the best sense, it becomes respectable.

There are many recognitions of this kind of prayer. In an ancient and beautiful book, the *Theologica Germanica,* we read that the purpose of prayer is that we should "be to the eternal goodness what his own hand is to a man." Each person has hidden energies which deserve to be released. Within every man dwell imprisoned splendors of hope, aspiration, and spiritual achievement. In fact, this particular path of prayer has been worn by the passage, through the ages, of all sorts of men and women who have sought and found an open way to religious truth. There are no sectarian barriers on this path. Jesus traveled it, but so, too, did Buddha, Laotse, and Gandhi. This is a journey which may be taken by any and all men. Each of the world's great religions has contributed to our knowledge of the terrain. This inward excursion to the growth and transformation of the human spirit is one of the truest marks of the universality of religion. In spite of all the external differences of the faiths by which men live, the inward pilgrimage is everywhere much the same. Aldous Huxley called it *The Perennial Philosophy.* Buddha named it *The Noble Eight Fold Path.* Others have called it simply "the way." On this journey no one needs to

be separated from his fellows by differences of doctrines. All
are friends and companions.

We are first made aware of our need for a deepening of
the inward life in various ways. Awareness may arise from
a haunting sense of dissatisfaction with ourselves as we are.
Or, we may become bored and weary with too much surface
activity, which leaves little or no time for thought and reflection. We may feel that there *must* be more comprehensive
meanings to life than those we have thus far discovered. Our
lives may receive a severe jolt, shaking us to the foundations;
so we pause and take stock. We ask questions about what we
are doing, and why we are doing it. We make an effort to
find out what our lives should mean, what they do mean,
and what they could mean.

Here, in this process of self-examination, the sifting and
judging of our desires goes on. Here we can slowly learn what
is one of the first and deepest lessons of religious growth:
that the stern demands of love, justice, and truth may well
run contrary to our personal desires. The deepest fulfillment
of our lives is *not* to be found in getting what we think we
want, but in giving what is needed and required. Here we
are made humble and, eventually, wise. Until a person has
felt and experienced this process, his religion has not really
begun to ripen. It does not much matter how it comes about,
in church or out, verbally or silently, mentioning God or not
mentioning God. What matters is that it *does* happen, and
that when it happens we know that we are involved in the
first, tentative steps of genuine prayer.

Quite rightly, psychologists tell us that these initial,
hesitant break-throughs are fraught with dangers. Self-examination alone, without further positive steps, can lead to
self-abasement, discouragement, and despair. We must push
beyond our all-too-evident weaknesses and failings. We must
find and recognize the strengths we have, and the hopes. This
is the *seeking* aspect of prayer, only it must be a seeking

which is disciplined and cleansed of narcissism. As Phillips Brooks expressed it: "Do not pray for easy lives. Pray to be stronger men. Do not pray for tasks equal to your powers. Pray for powers equal to your tasks." Once entered upon the inward journey, we have an obligation to seek the strength and courage equal to great tasks. This is the positive part of prayer, its outreach. Much honesty is required. There is plenty of space for settlement but none for sentimentality in this kind of praying. "Who rises from prayer a better man," says George Meredith, "his prayer is answered." Only by keenest searching, testing, and criticizing does anyone ever arise from prayer "a better man." Nowhere is the well-ordered mind more important than in prayer.

Finally, there is the aspect of patience. Lives conditioned to constant activity do not readily appreciate the value and necessity of simply waiting in silence, in expectation, in appreciation of things to come. One of the most colorful and promising aspects of the human mind is its ability to experience sudden flashes of insight and clarity. All at once a sense of direction emerges out of chaos. Formidable obstacles melt away. A decision is suddenly plain. Norbert Wiener, a true scientific genius, told his students that solutions to seemingly insoluble problems frequently came to him in the dead of night, when his mind was presumably at rest.

Sometimes we seem to have nothing to offer but our perplexity, our indecision, our confusion. Then, out of the silence, the waiting, the expectation, and the appreciation of things to come, a light breaks through. A prayer is answered? Yes, but not in a supernatural or magical sense. It is simply true that some of the most important moral decisions and spiritual discoveries come upon us with a kind of surprise and wonder when we are receptive and ready to use them.

These, then, are aspects of prayer which recommend themselves to a person like myself, who does not hesitate to register his distaste for prayers seeking wealth, rain, victory, safety, fishhooks, or the discomfiting of enemies.

Prayer based on self-examination, on an honest ordering of our minds, and on the ability to wait in expectation and appreciation upon our untapped and unrevealed spiritual resources, is, to me, respectable prayer. In the words of my colleague, Lon Ray Call: "Prayer doesn't change things, but it changes people and people change things. Let us pray."

Security

I am not a Unitarian Universalist because it gives me security. No one should try this religion for a security. Carl Sandburg explains what I mean in his poem "Man the Moon Shooter":

... ever the prophets are a dime a dozen
and man goes on a moon shooter.

The shapes of change
ai ai they take their time
asking what the dawn asks
giving the answers evening gives
till tomorrow moves in
saying to man the moon shooter
'Now I am here—now read me—
give me a name.'

Man, in Sandburg's eyes, is a "moon shooter," a restless, roving, inquisitive creature of change, ever striving for an unknown future. There is no real stopping place, no status quo. There are always the next shapes of change to come.

What about rest for the weary soul? Change is inspiring, exciting. But man is also a creature in need of peace. What place is there for peace? Not only do we need the thrill of progress, of movement, but there is yet another need in us: the need for things dependable, things reliable, things steady, things which stand fast while we think our way through the enigmas, puzzles and conundrums of a swiftly changing world.

Sandburg raises an ancient problem. Man is, indeed, a moon shooter, but he also longs for solid ground beneath his feet. Where will he find that solid ground? In what thoughts, what beliefs, what faiths? In the midst of change, on what can man depend?

Robert Frost warmed to these questions in his narrative poem "The Star-Splitter," which tells the story of New Hampshireman, Brad McLaughlin, described by Frost as a "hugger-mugger" farmer.

> He burned his house down for the fire insurance
> And spent the proceeds on a telescope
> To satisfy a life-long curiosity
> About our place among the infinities.

At first, Frost tells us, there was some mean laughter, but soon the townsfolk began to reflect:

> If one by one we counted people out
> For the least sin, it wouldn't take us long
> To get so we had no one left to live with,
> For to be social is to be forgiving.

So, Brad McLaughlin bought his telescope and took a job as ticket agent for the Concord railroad, a job which gave him leisure for stargazing. He and his friend, the narrator, spent countless hours in the evening looking up "the brass barrel, velvet black inside, at a star quaking in the other end."

> We've looked and looked, but after all where are we?
> Do we know any better where we stand,
> And how it stands between the night tonight
> And a man with a smoky lantern chimney?
> How different from the way it ever stood?

Frost has pondered the questions about security and raised some new ones about serenity. Is it abnormal to want serenity? Can man be a moon shooter and still be serene? Can he find serenity in the stars or in anything outside his own being? If we cannot find serenity in the stars, can we find it in what the stars help us to learn about ourselves?

Let's go back again to that solid ground beneath our feet. In a religious sense, where are we likely to find it? In a religion of blind faith? Does this universe make life easier for us if we subscribe to the right creed, or learn the approved catechism, or study *Science and Health With Key to the Scriptures?* No, we say; it is not that kind of universe! Where then is security? Where the solid ground? If we really want an answer, a strong answer—one which doesn't try to blink the facts, or sentimentalize the realities—we can hardly do better than the tough thoughts of the tender-spirited Emerson: "Nothing is secure but life, transition, the energizing spirit. No love can be bound by oath or covenant to secure it against a higher love. No truth so sublime but it may be trivial tomorrow in the light of new thoughts. People wish to be settled; only in so far as they are unsettled is there any hope. . . ." And then Emerson quotes Oliver Cromwell as having said: "A man never rises so high as when he knows not whither he is going."

Obviously Emerson offers us little in the way of comfortable assurance. If "a man never rises so high as when he knows not whither he is going," most of us would have little trouble sailing free to the moon. Perhaps there is more to this than first meets the eye. Possibly it is in just such a time as our own, when it is impossible to know exactly where we are going, that we are literally forced by our problems and challenges to rise to new heights of achievement. Is it, after all, so important to know exactly where we are going, as long as we know the general direction in which we want to travel and the stronger, warmer faith we will need for the journey?

What more should we ask than the solid reliance of this belief, that somehow, because of the nature of what is required of us, we will respond, and will rise higher than we dreamed possible? If only a nobler humanity is equal to our present problems, then a nobler humanity we will be.

By no stretch of the imagination can this be called *security*. At least, it is not the kind of security which makes us feel snug and safe and protected against the barbs and thrusts of life. "Nothing is secure," says Emerson, "but life, transition, the energizing spirit." With this perspective we achieve a larger conception of religion. If we would find solid ground beneath our feet, we must have courage enough to give up our illusions of a protected life and accept our role as the servants of life, the agents of transition, the children of the energizing spirit: subject to all the shocks and stresses of life, but confident and buoyant through them all. This is religion at its greatest, not as a petty search for protection, or as a pinched hope of buying God off, but as the wonderful adventure of life itself; as great as a world which is dying and a world which is waiting to be born; as great as a soul which sees clearly what is required of it, and rises confidently to meet the future. This kind of religion *is* solid ground, and when we have discovered it, nothing can take it away.

What of serenity? We will not find it in the tranquillizers of the spirit, or in the counterfeit "peace of mind" gambits. Many of the books and pulpit recitals devoted these days to the search for serenity are directed at those who seek an easy way out. There is no easy way. The road to serenity is as rigorous as any we will ever travel. Serenity comes not from escaping the realities of life, but from being in the midst of them. The best human beings have always been those who achieved serenity by taking upon themselves the pain, the fear, the suffering, the dark passions and guilts of man's inhumanity to man. Whether we speak of a Catholic St. Francis or a Unitarian Jane Addams, we know that this is the truth of the matter. No one comes by serenity cheaply. To gain it, a person has to meet its requirements; he has to do the deeds and make the choices which bring serenity. For each of us it means making the right choices, the difficult choices, the demanding choices. No one can consciously choose the lower against the higher and know inner peace. Serenity is involvement in the unserene.

We began with two poets: one who speaks of man the moon shooter, and another who spins yarn about a farmer who sought solace in an ill-gotten telescope. We found them raising profound questions about security and serenity. In each case, the answer came back "Look within!" The tasks of finding solid ground, of making peace with oneself, these are inner tasks in the midst of change, challenge, and conflict. If we break beneath our burdens, we break from within. If we master life, that mastery also comes from within. All of life is change, and we cannot escape it. We look for strength, peace, and where do we find them but in a sense of being useful, of being whole, of being warmly members of the human race, of doing what is called for by the deep nature of life.

TEN

A FACE TO THE FUTURE

*Thus we have to eat a second time from the tree of knowledge
in order to recover our state of innocence....*

HEINRICH VON KLEIST, *On the Puppet Show*

IN a recent twenty-four hour period, one set of officials
announced that we had developed a new world-wide radio-
monitoring detection system, and another group reported
that we had launched into the widest orbit thus far a scientific satellite which will provide unprecedented information
about the earth and its atmospheres. I firmly believe that in
the long run, the second of these accomplishments will provide the larger rewards. This latest adventure of a satellite,
happily a successful one, is the tradition of man's oldest and
greatest glory. The never-ending effort to widen the scope of
human knowledge is one of the profoundest features distinguishing man from other forms of life. Not by accident
did Prometheus and his discovery of fire become the most
honored of the Greek myths.

Every age repeats in its own way the story of discovery.
Archimedes, Euclid, Copernicus, Galileo, Descartes, Newton,
Einstein, Bohr, Salk—they tread in sequence across the horizons of history, impelled by the restless, driving force, to push
back the boundaries of our knowledge. This force is at the
heart of most of the breathtaking transformations of how
people actually live. It is forever placing new weapons in our

200

hands to be used against the ancient enemies: disease, famine, and ignorance. Always there are those who want to know, who cannot rest until they do know, and what is discovered is then passed on to others.

Our generation, and the one before us, have known more explosive surges of knowledge than any previous ones. The dimensions of thinking have leaped outward. We are obliged day by day to alter and readjust our conceptions in line with novel developments in the laboratory and the proving ground. New words are piled into our vocabularies, and these words go beyond linguistics because they represent new realizations and thoughts. We can never go back to the world of our grandfathers. We can never be the same again.

Even so, we are not at the conclusion of a process, but in its midstream. We are at a threshold, not an end. More than ever, we must become aware of what is happening. We must keep abreast and in tune. Above all, we must make certain that our moral sense is kept in balance with this surging knowledge. We must learn how to use the new means to the highest ends.

In the light of this, I look about me and am appalled at much of what passes currently for religious inspiration. One example is the sprawling Biblical spectacle on film entitled *The Big Fisherman*. Sunday schools all over the land busily sent hordes of children and parents to feast their eyes on this Cinema-Scope tableau. For what? Not entertainment, which it might legitimately be called. No, they were sent for spiritualization. In this age of Sputniks, Vanguards, Explorers, fission, fusion, and astrophysics, how can anyone be really deepened in spirit by a parade in full color of unhistorical Biblical vignettes and miracles? If it is offered as entertainment, no one can object. *The Big Fisherman* was not promoted as entertainment. We were told, instead, that it was "a magnificent experience in reverence." If ever there was an example of pouring old wine into new bottles, this is it. It

will not do. Unless there is a new *approach* to religion, not
the same old pre-scientific credulities in modern Hollywood
costumes, there can be no creative and significant role for the
spiritual life in today's and tomorrow's world. Whatever the
origins, whatever the past contributions, religion cannot expect to remain a vital force unless it lives in the mental
framework of modern life. I am a Unitarian Universalist because I feel that I am free in this church to foster what seems
to me to be religion's most crucial concern: to express itself
in terms which are truly designed to keep the moral sense
in balance with the complexities of advancing knowledge.

This position can be forthrightly taken. No concessions
need to be made to anti-intellectualism or obscurantism. It is
not necessary, in order to keep the laymen peaceful in their
pews, to mouth a lot of meaningless phrases which are completely incompatible with human-centered free thinking.
Liberal religion, like every phase of modern knowledge, is in
transition. Rather than trying to return to the theological
cradles of the past, it is moving on. We have left the authori-
tarian God behind and are reaching out for expanded, spiritualized conceptions of God which are in keeping with an
expanding, spiritualized universe. We have left the ancient
magic and miracles of supernaturalism behind and are striving to understand the natural miracles of mind, energy,
evolution, and human development. We have left behind the
dark traditions of original sin and metaphysical blight and
are trying to grow an awareness of the true sufficiencies and
insufficiencies of man.

The primary problem of modern religion is creative religious behavior, and in this respect Unitarian Universalists
reflect one of the most significant changes taking place in
contemporary thinking. We are discovering that there is something in ourselves—and in life as a whole—far more meaningful than conscious mind and measurable energy. We owe a
monumental debt to Sigmund Freud for opening our eyes

to some of this deeper understanding, but he was a pioneer, and therefore only a beginner. His field was medicine and his chief interest was, understandably, in the cure of disease. By discovering the depths beneath the levels of consciousness, he felt that he had come upon central clues to the causes of mental illness. Freud's chief domain was the "unconscious repressed." He became absorbed with the problems of loosing man from the chains in his subconscious. It was essentially a task of dealing with negative forces.

Freud's accomplishments were germinal. What is taking place today is a projection from his discoveries into the exciting positive forces which live in our depths.

In the October, 1958, issue of *The Saturday Evening Post*, Aldous Huxley advocated the use of chemical drugs to heighten human vigor and intelligence. Without going into the moral or medical merits of his proposal, we should all be intensely interested in Huxley's corollary claim that most of us function at about fifteen per cent of our potential capacity. Whatever the exact percentage, it would be foolish to deny that we operate far beneath full competence most of the time. What we are increasingly discovering is that there are vast, unused propensities to growth within us. These are the forces which are capable of determining the directions, and providing the possibilities, of human development. They are the astonishing potentialities of ourselves. It would not be wide of the mark to call these emerging possibilities *depth religion*.

At our present point in civilization, many forces militate against a realization of depth religion. Organized religions themselves are frequently the worst offenders, treating man not as a spiritually creative being, but as an object to be "saved." To use the phraseology of Martin Buber, the individual is dealt with not as a *Thou* (a person), but as an *It* (a thing). The natural tendency of most people is to behave as they are treated, and to treat others in a similar manner.

Thus does a man come to think of himself as though he
operates according to the same mechanical laws which gov-
ern his automobile. If he needs a car, he goes to a dealer to get
one. If he needs religious inspiration, he goes to a church to
get it. If something goes wrong with his car, he goes to the
garage to have it repaired by experts. If something is bother-
ing his spirit, he goes to a church to have it set right by
experts. But a man is not an automobile. He becomes like an
automobile only when he loses faith in his own inner capacities. Then he grinds along, a machine in a world of machines. Religion is external to him. It "fixes him up."

Essentially the same effect is felt from the violent contrasts
and crosscurrents of modern society. They disrupt us, alienate us from a sense of intimacy with our world, and eventually they alienate us from ourselves. The result is that we no
longer live our lives from the inside out, but in terms of the
various stereotypes the world imposes upon us. We make
machines that act more and more like men, while men act
more and more like machines.

If you are a "thinking man," you smoke Viceroys. If you
are a "man's man," you puff Marlboros. If yours is a "happy
family"—in the midwest—you go Krogering. And, of course,
"if you pray together you stay together." Presumably no one
ever smokes just because he enjoys it; no one goes shopping
merely as a wearisome but practical necessity; no one prays
simply because he feels some deep, personal, inner need to do
so. There is always the underlying assumption that we are
waiting around for the proper image to be created—a syn-
thetic self—into which we can happily fit. From the world of
marketing there recently came this gemlike observation of a
noted commercial analyst: "The solution to marketing problems is not necessarily one of giving consumers what they
want, but rather to make consumers want what we, the mar-
keters, want them to want."

This is a remarkably succinct summary of the *Thou* and *It* dilemma.

Simplify! Simplify! said Thoreau, who could put down twenty-eight dollars for a refuge on Walden Pond and regain his soul by turning his back on the world. Thoreau, let it be added, had no family to support. Anyway, twenty-eight dollars would not buy much of a retreat these days.

Our predicament goes far deeper than it did in Thoreau's time, and it has little to do with the pocketbook or the price structure. It involves the depth areas of the self: feelings, emotions, values, conscience, reason. These are being crowded out by *The Big Fisherman,* the big evangelist, the big church, the big government, the big industry, the big union, the big rat race.

The function of depth religion in all of this is to take its stand for the inner man, to rescue the *Thou* from its *It* status, and to guide the *Thou* to the riches of untapped treasure within the depths and heights of man himself.

As a Unitarian Universalist, I dedicate my life to the *truly* creative religious behavior of the *truly* modern man, who is learning to live in close touch with his times, who feels the impact of its problems, and who undertakes to resolve them both within himself and in his activities in the world.

We live amidst a mass production of events and things. They perpetually crowd our vision and consciousness with an oppressive closeness of undifferentiated details and complexities. These contrasts and discordancies *can* crush our will to respond with feeling, with sensitivity, with a discriminating consciousness of values. We can cease to be genuinely aware of what we see and hear. Our emotions and critical judgments can become so shrunken that our eventual attitude to what is going on in the world is flat and indifferent. With machines to take care of our machines, with priests, evangelists, and faith healers to take care of our souls, with vast, impersonal bureaucracies to take care of our education, economics, politics, and foreign relations, we can lapse into complete and total *Itness*.

I cannot and will not accept that the human spirit will have it so. The basic life stuff is a moving toward goals which are built into the nature of the organism. We humans have in-built goals which are not so feeble as to be deterred and destroyed by the complexities our expanding knowledge and numbers have brought us. The essential meaning of our lives —even in the midst of all that is so new and calamitous—is not in becoming part of a mechanical interplay of mechanical forces, but to seek more profoundly than ever in our thoughts and activities the evolving goals of our emerging spiritual selves.

Our present state is oppressive, but it is not the end of the road. The cosmos beckons. There is in us the stuff out of which new and glorious epochs may be fashioned. I am a Unitarian Universalist because I would feel silly being part of any religious movement which faces contemporary life and problems with a basic longing for the old theological mangers; because I want to ally myself with others who are consciously striving to explore and reveal man's creative heights and depths; because I share with Wordsworth this holy injunction: "So build we up the being that we are."

The mysterious life-germ, of which we are remarkable manifestations, possesses a buoyant urge forward, which in human terms can be fulfilled only as we both know and transcend ourselves. I am a Unitarian Universalist because our religion zestfully celebrates human reason, and it is reason's task to point our way, to seek out the right direction of travel. It is by reason that we know what ought to be. It is by reason that we find meaning in moral decision. It is by reason that we grow responsible. It is by reason that we come to care for ideals, for standards, for criteria, for the arts of logical distinction and cultivated judgment. By reason we understand the meaning of self-giving, and the importance of having a self to give. By reason we see that the struggle for the life of others is as fundamental as struggle for the life of self; that interest in the life of others is deeply woven into the fabric of the life-process; that we are not born to be little incarnate centers of selfishness. The self is private, personal, and precious, but it is not isolated from other selves. It is wholly unique, but it is never the exclusive center of the universe.

All this we learn and know because the faculty of reason is our birthright. When loved and used, reason affirms that we are human because we are capable of being deepened, and that until we are deepened, we cannot know joy or fulfillment.

These are bleak and vulgar days for the human spirit, but they will be fatal days only if this generation, unlike all others, is without stalwarts who distill from the very essence of the predicament the wonder of its resolution. I believe that Unitarian Universalism provides a very special place for such stalwarts. I am proud to call it the religion of my heart and mind.

INDEX